Preaching with Humanity

Preaching with Humanity

A practical guide for today's church

Geoffrey Stevenson and Stephen Wright

CHURCH HOUSE
PUBLISHING

Prelude

Geoffrey Stevenson

We believe in preaching. 'The preaching of the Word of God *is* the Word of God', so ran the Second Helvetic Confession.[1] Only we want to be real about an enterprise that is undertaken by humans for fellow humans, with the potential for all the glory, misuse, joy and sorrow, seriousness and silliness that goes with being human. Therefore we have chosen not to begin this book by highlighting the crisis in our pulpits today and then going on to promise that in these pages you will find all the answers to all the problems. We believe in preaching, but we are (we like to think) realistic.

If you ask preachers about what they think they are doing, and then ask listeners about their experience, you sometimes get the impression that they have not been part of the same event. It seems there was not one sermon, but many – at least as many sermons as there were listeners, plus the one the preacher preached, plus the one the preacher was *hoping* to preach, not to mention the one that *should* have been preached if the preacher had listened more closely to the text and to the congregation and to the Holy Spirit! Actually this fragmentation of meaning is the challenge facing any preacher, and when communion through communication is achieved in a way that breaches the walls that separate us from another, and from God, then it is a miracle of sorts. Certainly the process remains shrouded in mystery. How God speaks and blesses and guides, how the Spirit confronts, convicts, and convinces, how people receive strength and comfort through a believing preacher's bare words is a source of wonder and thanksgiving. So we do believe in preaching as a gift to the Church, though it is one whose workings are not fully understood. Perhaps they never will be. One reason is that words are so slippery and sinuous, and language so flimsy a container for our deepest experiences and apprehensions of truth. Another reason is that God has only revealed a tiny proportion of himself or herself in ways that our minds can grasp. The third-century theologian Origen called this the principle of accommodation, like a schoolmaster adapting his language so that his children may understand him. This should in turn give a 'provisionality' to our efforts to preach, but it also makes preaching one of the most exciting and awesome callings in the world.

We believe in preaching *with humanity*, and as long as you are not fixed in your mind about sermons being fixed at 12 minutes or 3 points or always ending with the cross or only deliverable from a pulpit (although we certainly approve of and have preached in all of these ways) then we can reasonably hope that there is something here to help you in the life-long process of becoming a preacher with humanity.

The best model for adult learning is usually considered these days to be that of the reflective practitioner. So this is a book of theory that expects to be put into practice, and of practice that needs to be reflected upon afterwards. Moreover, adults do not in general learn well by being told what to think and do, so this is a book that should raise as many questions as it answers. In sum, it is up to the learner to seek answers to questions raised by practice and by reflection on that practice, and we hope that process will take preachers into some of the further resources that we recommend at the end. Here are some of the questions we ask ourselves about preaching:

- What, for example, is the challenge of preaching within a culture that is so dominated by the visual, from television and cinema to YouTube™ and web page graphics? How can live speech be as effective as polished presentations in the mass media?

- How does the context of worship shape preaching, and who are the 'players' involved in a preaching event? Won't God be able to speak by his Holy Spirit if he chooses to, no matter what the preacher does? And how does a preacher get from the scriptural text to a 'preachable' message? What are good ways to prepare a sermon?

- What kind of personal qualities do I require or must I develop in order to be a preacher? More practically, can I preach with the speaking skills that I have, or must I develop the so-called parsonical voice? Can I be myself in the pulpit, or do I have to have some sort of artificial, 'actorish' personality?

- How can the congregation be involved in the preaching event? How can I create sermons that address the real needs and day-to-day concerns of my congregation? Will I ever get anything more than 'Nice sermon, minister' at the door? Should I care?

Finally, we raise what we consider to be crucial questions about the place of preaching in a 'mission-shaped Church':

- Should the nature, tone and content of preaching reflect the growing understanding of church leadership as being called to 'mission management'? Alternatively, does this mean that preachers need to move from 'in-house talk' to 'seeker sensitivity' and apologetics in their sermons?

And do I really have to use PowerPoint™ to reach listeners who receive just about everything they know through the TV?

We do not offer definitive answers to these questions, but we have tried in this book to contribute to the developing understanding of preaching in Christ's Church.

We offer this book with a great sense of 'standing on the shoulders of giants', and we admit to sometimes borrowing their clothes (despite the size mismatch). We offer it with 'provisionality' for it is not the last word by any means, and it is, like a sermon, rooted in the time and place it was written. But we offer it confidently because we believe that the Church needs preachers who embrace their humanity, who believe in preaching the word of God, and who are, in the words of Martin Luther, 'willing to risk body, blood, wealth, honour to preach'.

1

The problems with 'preaching'

Stephen Wright

On a freezing, foggy winter morning in a busy London suburb just before Christmas, I saw a preacher who had taken up position on a patch of green. Against the dull roar of buses rolling past, amid the fumes of exhaust, and in the face of massive indifference from harassed shoppers bent only on getting into the next warm store, or getting home as quickly as possible, she shouted at the top of her voice, with variations on a theme: 'Jesus is the only Saviour! You must give your life to him if you want to go to heaven!'

A few minutes later I was at my destination: the offices of an organization running Speed Awareness Workshops. A few weeks previously, I had been caught speeding on camera. As an alternative to endorsement of licences, the police were inviting those whose offence involved an excess of only a few miles per hour to a workshop, designed to refresh drivers' minds about legal and practical aspects of speed limits and to provoke thought about the possible consequences of breaking them. Apparently the scheme has been successful in reducing the rate of re-offending. It was an interesting and worthwhile event. As part of his introductory preamble, the workshop leader, an experienced driving instructor, assured us: 'I'm not going to preach to you – that wouldn't do any good.'

Having a particular interest in the Christian practice we usually term 'preaching', I was struck by the conjunction of these two events. Together they point to the core problems that both our society and the Church itself have with the practice, and with talking about it, today.

The first problem is to do with _context_. What is the right setting for public speech about our faith? And if we can find the right setting, how should such speech fit into it? The street preacher screaming the gospel at careworn Christmas shoppers epitomizes what many find difficult and counter-intuitive about the very idea of preaching. Not only does such preaching seem to have very little effect. Most people probably suspect it is actually counter-productive. It gives the impression of a Church whose only concern is to trumpet its message and has little or no care for the people to whom it is ostensibly communicating. In this sense, the driving instructor seemed to have grasped something which the street evangelist had not: there's not much point in 'preaching' to strangers who are probably not disposed to like what you say.

Thus, we tend to think, the most effective form of preaching is likely to be in a context where at least some of the hearers are 'with' the preacher; in a context, moreover, where the words of the preacher alone are not carrying the whole weight of the message. In other words, in the context of corporate worship, where the Christian story is being told and celebrated through a variety of different means, 'preaching' seems to fit better. In an atmosphere of faith, preaching is more likely to engender more faith.

And indeed it is 'preaching' within the context of regular Christian worship with which this book is concerned. However, as soon as we have limited it to this context, we are faced with a further set of problems.

On the one hand we may secretly wonder if this limitation of preaching is 'copping out'. The clichéd slogan that is likely to pop up here is 'preaching to the converted'. Isn't it an easy option simply to preach among those who already share your faith, or at least are in sympathy with it? What about the millions who never darken the door of a church – isn't it our business to be trying to reach them? Aren't we focusing our energies on simply confirming an ever-decreasing number of people in their faith, while ignoring those who most need to hear our message?

Responses to such concerns will emerge in the course of this book. But what should be immediately clear is that we cannot talk sensibly about preaching today without considering the wider context in which it takes place, indeed the nature and calling of the Church itself. We will explore particularly the connection of preaching with the contexts of mission, worship, education and pastoral care.

On the other hand we hear voices telling us that even among the faithful in church, preaching is an authoritarian activity ill-fitted to the context of contemporary society. The implication is that those who engage in it may be exercising power inappropriately over their hearers. Perhaps the hearers are happily colluding with this, or maybe they are inwardly rebelling against it. More occasional visitors – so the thought runs – are unlikely to be impressed with a form of communication so quaint and unlike other forms of public discourse with which they are familiar. Responses to these concerns, too, will emerge in due course. But first we turn to the other main problem with 'preaching' highlighted by my opening story.

This is the problem of *language* – that is, the word 'preaching' itself. The throwaway comment of the workshop leader is replicated countless times in everyday speech. 'Preaching' is a pejorative term. It names an activity seen as ineffectual at best, abusive at worst. Close synonyms would be 'hectoring', 'lecturing' (another potentially neutral word, now often used pejoratively), even 'haranguing'. This is an activity seen as designed to induce guilt, which it often succeeds in. It does not *communicate* in the sense of building on and establishing a bond between speaker and hearer. In contemporary Britain, it has recently picked up extra negative connotations from reports of firebrand Islamic preachers – no doubt a small minority – who contribute to the 'radicalization' of young Muslims.

The street preacher and the workshop leader form an instructive contrast here. The former was doing exactly what the latter meant when he said he was not going to 'preach'. And the latter was true to his word. He did not 'preach'. He laid out facts and situations in a clear, dispassionate way, but with clear sympathy with his audience and a desire actually to move us to change, to think more carefully about our driving and to translate those thoughts into practice. He allowed opportunity for interaction and feedback. There was a palpable sense in the room that he was succeeding. To be sure, maybe only those willing to learn had signed up for the workshop; but learn, I'm sure, most of us did.

Against this backdrop, it's easier to see what we are up against when we try to talk about 'preaching' in a Church context. On the one hand, we have no other word in our language that expresses quite so accurately the classic Christian activity of public proclamation of our faith. ('Proclaiming' is perhaps the nearest alternative, but it has some of the same disadvantages as 'preaching', while lacking the latter's general familiarity.) On the other hand, ask the vast majority of Christians whether they are in favour of 'preaching' in the sense implied by the workshop leader's use of the term, and they will give an unequivocal 'no'. Define a word so negatively, and what do you expect?

Indeed, as authors we too are against 'preaching' when defined like this. Yet we, and thousands of others around the country – not to mention across the world – are engaged in 'preaching', in its classic sense, regularly through the year, as both preachers and listeners. It is a practice common to all the major Christian traditions and honoured by them. It would be ridiculous to suggest that all such regular occurrences of 'preaching', widely varied as they are, entail collusion in an oppressive event by preacher and listeners, or to deny that many find preaching (at least some of the time) wholesome, nurturing and faith-building. But in thinking through how we may work together to redeem the activity from sometimes justified ill-repute into which it has fallen in some quarters, this is the bind that many thoughtful Christian leaders find themselves in. Putting it as sharply as possible: how do you preach without preaching?

The purpose of this book is to explore this question. There are those who answer it simply by saying, 'You can't'. To this way of thinking, the practice of preaching is so irredeemably tainted by its negative associations that it needs not reformation, but death. We do not believe the answer to be as simple as this. While wholeheartedly embracing the use of a range of forms for Christian communication, we wish to continue to affirm the unique place of preaching in Christian witness and its potential for Christian formation.

Later we will outline in more detail the reasons for this, and explore ways in which the practice can be life-giving rather than deadly. Here let us be content to say that many of the techniques used by the leader of the Speed Awareness Workshop, and the philosophy lying behind them (with the eschewal of 'preaching'), are precisely the kind of thing being expounded and recommended, within an explicitly theological framework, by many thinkers and practitioners in the field of homiletics (the study of preaching). Our hope here, then, is not to try to prop up or rehabilitate any form of authoritarian or oppressive discourse, but to point to ways in which new life might be given to an honoured and (we believe) indispensable practice of the Church. If your own preaching ministry is sometimes plagued by doubt as to whether it is worthwhile, we trust that you will be encouraged. If you have confidence in it, we trust that you will find fresh ideas for exercising it effectively. If you think that 'preaching' in all senses has had its day, we trust that you will at least listen to an alternative viewpoint.

A good place to start is by placing the traditional practice of preaching in the light of some of the key dimensions of the Church's life with which it intersects: mission, worship, education and pastoral care. This will enable us to glimpse more clearly the reasons why the discussion of preaching is fraught with difficulties today, and why the practice itself is often condemned outright, or at least damned with faint praise. We shall also start to see how a renewal of the practice cannot be contemplated in isolation but must be considered in tandem with developments in these (and other) areas.

Preaching and mission

In recent years the Church has been regularly called to recover its sense of being a missionary movement rather than a set of static institutions.[1] The recent report from the Church of England, *Mission-shaped Church*,[2] documented a variety of creative ways in which Christians are working beyond traditional structures and boundaries to fulfil the commission of Christ. To recover our missionary identity, it is argued, is not fundamentally a matter of boosting numbers or influence. It is returning to our roots.

For our purposes, one of the intriguing things about this report is that it never mentions preaching. One can see the reason for this. Where the Church in its mission is breaking out of the structure of formal 'congregational' gatherings, and meeting in cell groups, pubs or cafés, then it is natural that the formality of a 'sermon' should be abandoned. Preaching is likely to be replaced by lively discussion. This is a good and natural development, surely in line with the missionary thrust of the Church from earliest times. However, this does not in itself mean that there is no place for preaching in the contemporary Church. *Mission-shaped Church* itself may hint at this when it acknowledges that only when a new 'expression of church' has a regular ministry of word and sacrament can it be recognized as a 'Church'.[3]

But this recognition that there is a natural evolution of new forms of Church life into something more structured and generally recognizable is telling. It fits with widely accepted understandings of the way organizations develop. In the case of the Church, it is crucial that there are discernible ways in which gatherings of Christians show their connectedness to the body of Christ across space and time. Along with Scripture, sacraments, prayer and authorized ministry, one such key mark is proclamation of the gospel – by some recognizable means!

Perhaps this gives us the clue as to how 'preaching' fits into a renewed vision of the Church as a missionary body. It is not 'front-line' mission and does not need to pretend to be. It is the fresh and faithful re-statement of the Christian gospel for each place and each generation, through which churches are sustained, renewed and reinvigorated to move out in ever-new missionary ventures. It is the place to which the missionaries return to rest awhile, as the disciples returned to Jesus.

There is, however, a broader concern about the place of preaching within a 'missionary' Church. This relates to the style and mode of public discourse in society at large.

We have already mentioned the anti-authoritarian mood of our dominant culture. In a recent interview, Pete Ward expresses it like this:

> In the culture at large, the idea that one person can tell other people what to believe is not seen as just boring or irrelevant. The imposition of belief is seen as a kind of violence and abuse. This means that preaching – to the extent that it implies telling people what to think – is seen as an act of an immoral person.[4]

Ward is surely correct about the atmosphere of suspicion of authority, of being told what to believe or do without a chance to have one's own say. The question we need to press is this. Rather than being a reason for not preaching at all, is this not a summons to us to return, if we have departed from it, to the humility, gentleness and vulnerability that should always have marked out our public speech as Christians? Is it a reminder that the authority of God – which we claim, in some sense, to be acting under when we preach – was supremely mediated to us in Christ the suffering servant? However, there is a further question to be pursued, which is whether our forms of preaching are still too shaped by an essentially 'modernist' culture based on the printed word and 'literary' forms of speech.

This culture has been profoundly influential on, and influenced by, the tradition of Protestantism with its focus on the Bible as a printed book. There has been important creative work exploring how preaching can adapt to what has been called a culture of 'secondary orality'. This is when our forms of communication remain deeply influenced by the organizing principles that came with the printed word, but have moved on to embrace a heady mix of imagistic and oral-technological means of interaction.[5] Today's young people say they are 'talking' online – typing words on a keyboard, but viewing them on screen (perhaps along with a picture of the person they are talking to), using pictorial 'emoticons' along with words, and using a definitely 'oral' version of syntax, grammar and spelling!

At this stage there are two points to be made about the proper impact of this so-called culture of 'secondary orality' upon preaching.

First, clearly as with every other way the Christian gospel intersects with culture, we should expect there to be both elements to embrace and elements to eschew. A wholesale rush to change our ways in order to be 'relevant' is to miss the point that a missionary engagement with culture must always be a *critical* engagement. Some aspects of 'secondary orality' may be seen to be vital to co-opt into the task of preaching (such as, maybe, sensitivity to the power of image or imagistic word). Other aspects may be seen as equally vital to avoid (the manipulation of pictures and language to 'sell' a product or idea in a deceptive manner).[6]

Secondly, don't imagine that by dispensing with preaching we avoid the challenge posed to the Church by contemporary forms of discourse. For the challenge fundamentally concerns all our public rhetoric as Christians: the language we use to each other and the language we use to be heard by the world. That 'language' is bound to entail both words and a whole network of symbolic objects and actions. This language comes to focus most obviously in corporate worship, and to that we turn now.

Preaching and worship

Patterns of worship deeply condition the preaching that happens within them. Preaching cannot usefully be considered apart from them. We will be exploring how preaching relates to some of the different traditions of worship in Chapter 2. For now here are two examples of this conditioning.

The first is the liturgical renewal movement. By the 1960s in the Church of England the Parish Communion was becoming well established as the central act of weekly worship. The sermon has come to be seen as part of the overall liturgical drama, rather than an event in its own right.[7] Its aim is to enable worshippers to enter fully into the enactment of the central events of redemption. The movement has also been influential in some of the Free Churches. Meanwhile the Roman Catholic Church, in the wake of the Second Vatican Council, has emphasized the importance of the ministry of the word alongside the eucharistic act. There has thus been an interesting convergence of preaching traditions with a focus on the context of liturgical celebration.

'Liturgical' preaching's great strength is its deep integration with the whole drama of worship; the drawback is that it may not allow enough time for the induction of less biblically literate congregations into the great truths of faith.

The second shift is the rise in 'all-age worship'. This prompts decisions about the ministry of the word. Will there be a sermon, accessible on different levels by a wide range of hearers? Will there be a sermon for adults while the children are engaged in some other activity? Or will there be no recognizable 'sermon' at all, but a highly participative, interactive service through which, it is hoped, people of all ages will be able to encounter God, and/or learn something about him?

Different patterns are likely to work best in different settings and traditions. It is clear that there is the potential both for a wonderful inclusivity, and for trivializing holy things in the name of accessibility to the young.[8]

Preaching and education

Important questions are posed to the practice of preaching today from the angle of education. If preaching is partly to be seen as a function of the Church's mission and worship, we should not reduce it to 'teaching', yet it has clearly had an important educational function in the past. But sometimes those committed to good educational practice and those committed to preaching can seem to be speaking different languages! A good example of how was found in two articles juxtaposed in *The Reader* magazine in Spring 2006.

On the one hand, in his article 'Preaching: a dying art?'[9] Leslie Griffiths, Superintendent Minister of Wesley's Chapel in London, Chairman of the College of Preachers, and a noted preacher and leader in Methodist and ecumenical circles wrote:

> The fact must surely be that preaching has to be held in the highest possible place in the life and worship of our churches whatever our own temperamental or theological or cultural assumptions about the nature of worship.

> Preaching must be passionate, urgent, persuasive, engaging, eye-opening, mind boggling, poetry, prophecy, uplifting and upsetting.

The second article, 'Readers – learning to help others to learn'[10] by Joanna Cox, national Adult Education Adviser for the Church of England, contained statements such as these:

> Widespread experience within the church suggests that preaching and 'telling' are the dominant educational approach, and that many have overlooked the need to train facilitators who can use processes that encourage others to engage actively with learning.

> A facilitator approaches the educational task with attitudes that differ from those of a preacher. To think in terms of learning rather than just of teaching makes (in grammatical terms) the learner the subject, rather than the object. This is a reminder of the importance of moving away from a hierarchical or paternalistic educational approach, towards one that sees the educator's involvement as a servant ministry.

> Successful facilitators also need to develop flexibility and be ready to relinquish control. This cannot be a situation where, as in the proverbial sermon, the teacher is in the pulpit 'six feet above contradiction'.

In their own terms, both articles are equally eloquent, helpful and persuasive. But their juxtaposition clearly sets us a task in elucidating the nature, purpose and appropriate forms of 'preaching'. Granted that, as we have seen, preaching is more than 'education', and therefore not to be directed by educationalist wisdom alone, what should the preacher learn from Cox's comments?

This again will be taken up in various ways through this book. But at this point it is worth underlining that everything she affirms about the need for a variety of ways for people to learn beyond simple 'instruction' has been regularly affirmed over recent decades by those working in the field of homiletics, that is, the study of *preaching*. Yes, *preaching* must be about not just 'telling', but enabling people to *hear*. As Fred Craddock, perhaps the most influential preaching writer of the latter part of the twentieth century, puts it: 'The goal is not to get something said but to get something heard'.[11]

Yes, *preaching* must not be hierarchical; *preaching* is a servant ministry, in which all God's people have a voice, because the preacher has listened deeply and comes forth to speak not from on high but from the midst of the congregation.[12]

Yes, *preachers* must be ready to relinquish control, and recognize that the word of God comes to, and is to be interpreted by, the people of God as a whole. Hence all the creative proposals we have heard from thinkers about preaching concerning ways in which a preacher can engage with a congregation: 'congregational exegesis',[13] 'the roundtable pulpit',[14] groups for 'conversational listening' with the preacher before the sermon event, and 'discerning, mutual listening' afterwards.[15]

This takes us back to the problem of language. An educationalist might say, 'if a "preacher" is engaged in the task in all these ways, he or she is no longer "preaching"!' So is this debate about the validity of 'preaching' just a semantic exercise? Could we not just drop the word 'preaching' and talk about education, facilitation or the like?

It is not as simple as that. The mood, style or method of preaching may need to change – in some places at least. But this does not entail abandoning an *activity* that is recognizably in continuity with what the Church has traditionally called 'preaching', as a central feature of its mission and worship. The whole activity may need to be re-envisioned – or, in Leslie Griffiths' words, 'rediscovered in all its glory'.[16] Indeed the nature and appropriate forms of this activity are precisely the subject of much contemporary homiletic study. But 'preaching' may turn out to be still the best word for it.

Preaching and pastoral care

Most sermons are preached by those who have some kind of pastoral oversight of their listeners, and the discussion of preaching will miss something vital if this area is not taken into account.

There are extreme views on this link that we can only deal with in passing here. At one end, there are those whose theology of preaching is so 'high' that pastoral care is *equated* with preaching. The minister has no need to visit the church members (so he or she thinks) – indeed, *should* not spend time on that! – because all the care they need is found in the 'medicine' of the preached word on Sunday! At the other end, there are those who view preaching as a minor matter compared to the 'real work' of individual pastoral encounter or community action. Maybe it was one such minister who responded to a colleague of mine, when the subject of preaching came up in conversation: 'Preaching? Oh, we don't do that any more.'

A much more common and persuasive view than either of these extremes is that preaching forms a seamless whole with pastoral care. It arises from the preacher's knowledge of those under his or her oversight, their joys and sorrows, and is a focal point for the discernment of God's presence in the community and his will for its future.[17] At the heart of both preaching and pastoral care is the act of interpretation, in which God's people, facilitated by those set apart for authorized ministry, seek to listen to his word as they try to make sense of Scripture in the light of today's world, and today's world in the light of Scripture. Thus when we are discussing preaching it is unhelpful to think of it as an event divorced from the wider reality of local church life, or to stereotype it as a solo performance. It is rather a regular focal point on a Christian community's pilgrimage.

Yet we must acknowledge that often this is not how it works out. A nurturing pastoral relationship is often far from evident in preaching. Take four brief examples:

Peter Phillips, director of the Tallis Scholars, gave the back page interview in the *Church Times* on 26 January 2007. Asked about sermons, his response was: 'I can't really stand sermons, but have certainly sat through a few in the course of my work . . . I find it odd that these clearly intelligent, gifted people can't get their point across.' The criticism implied here from a distinguished musician is that though the preachers seem to have something to say, they either lack the skill to put it over or have simply not prepared well enough. Of course, this raises questions not only about selection and training of preachers but also about their own commitment to their task.

Our second example is about the content of the message. Sometimes preachers are 'given the floor' who simply have a very inadequate grasp of Christian theology and principles of handling the Bible. This may go hand-in-hand with a glib over-dependence on the Holy Spirit – perhaps even with the claim of prophetic inspiration. The problem here is not the *form* of preaching but the ecclesial process whereby someone is allowed to voice the Christian message in a public gathering. The public space of Christian worship can end up being abused for the attempted imposition of eccentric private opinions. This situation highlights the importance of a trained, authorized and representative ministry able to articulate the faith for today.

Thirdly, there is the question of the preacher's posture or attitude towards the congregation. Twice recently I have been talking to highly intelligent Christians, exercising distinctive and crucial ministries, who voiced their concerns about the preaching they regularly hear. One singled out a particular preacher and sermon because 'for the first time in ages, I felt I was being treated as an adult in church'. The other commented that in her experience, preaching could easily lead to the infantilization of the hearers: they become trapped in a situation of over-dependency, as it were in a child–parent relationship to the preacher, and are not given the space to grow up spiritually. Of course, one consequence is that sooner or later, many will start to rebel. From the pastoral point of view, preaching may connive in a supposedly 'Christian' culture that squashes legitimate and vital questioning.

Finally – hype. A mature Christian woman recently heard a sermon at her local church as a part of a series on 'mission'. 'How was it?' I asked. 'OK, but it didn't fire me up' she answered. She went on: 'The trouble is that these series get so hyped up in advance – then when it comes, it's nothing special.' Behind this case there is a deeper and wider issue: the use of 'preaching' to exhort congregations to special efforts of one kind or another. In principle this is an appropriate part of the pastoral relationship: the pastor, or a visitor as in this case, is seeking to exercise motivational leadership.[18] However, the problem often seems to be that pastor-preacher-leaders have little sense of how quickly exhortation and 'hype' on its own leaves hearers cold and worn out. They forget that what warms the heart and gives light to the eyes and a spring in the step for God's service is undiluted, unconditional good news. That is why the gospel in all its many-splendoured richness must be at the heart of a renewal of preaching, not more tub-thumping 'hype'.

Preaching with humanity

Our title, then, gives the clue to the kind of preaching we wish to describe, advocate, aspire to and facilitate. It is preaching *with* humanity – *with* our fellow human beings of all types, not 'to' them or 'at' them from a height or a distance, as if we were superior or different. It is preaching with *humanity* – 'humane' in all the glory of what it is to be in the image of God, being renewed by his grace in Christ.

But there's another complication when we talk about 'preaching'. For different individuals and church traditions, the word can describe significantly different kinds of event. Understanding our own tradition of preaching and that of others is very important as we try to get a grip on what we are doing. So in the next chapter we'll drop in on some fairly 'typical' recent services (not that there really is such a thing!) and try to understand what is going on in the preaching.

2

Preaching in worship today

Stephen Wright

The word 'preaching' acts as a label for a multitude of different scenarios (and, some would say, sins!). In Chapter 1 I suggested that it is unhelpful to think about 'preaching' apart from a range of contexts with which it is linked: mission, worship, education, pastoral care. In this chapter we'll focus on how it connects to those contexts in a range of ordinary church settings.

All these examples are fictionalized versions of actual services I've attended. I want to show how each of them 'makes sense' within a particular worshipping tradition and the theology and spirituality which shapes it. I also want to point to natural limitations of the various kinds of preaching discussed, and to natural strengths on which practitioners can capitalize.

This is not meant to be an exercise of detached sociological description, to be skipped by those uninterested in that sort of thing; nor a piece of unsavoury ecclesiastical stereotyping. Rather, I want here to highlight two realities above all. First, that preaching is not the rightful preserve of only one or another Christian tradition, but has an authentic and distinctive home, and a particular character, in all of them. Secondly, that the very variety of events labelled 'preaching' should lead us to ask carefully what a particular preaching event is meant to *do* in a particular setting.

It may be that much suspicion of preaching, and much poor practice, stem from a failure to grasp these realities. If 'preaching' is seen as something done by 'them' (down the road), but as 'not really our thing', it's no wonder that 'we' don't work at it too hard; and the mediocre preaching that results then reinforces the original sense of alienation. Or if 'preaching' is seen as something unchangeable in form and mood, such that a preacher can bring the same content and style to any church in which they happen to speak, this too gives it a bad name, because the preacher has not grasped the fundamental importance of *context* to *communication*.

Most readers will be familiar with something of the origins and ethos of the preaching tradition within which they are naturally 'at home'. So in tracing the background of the following scenarios my aim is not to give a history lesson, but rather to prompt critical questioning about your own preaching tradition, and encourage you to explore insights from others. What are the things 'your' kind of preaching does naturally and well? What are the strengths to celebrate and build on? What are the shortcomings that it may have to work hard to compensate for? What may you be able to learn from other traditions, without compromising the integrity of your own?

Example 1

It's an evening eucharistic service in a Roman Catholic church. It's out in the country, but it's the only Catholic church for miles around, and there's a congregation of about 130 of a mixture of ages, including some children. The service follows a standard liturgical order, in which members of the congregation take an active role, doing readings and leading intercessions. There are three hymns that in various ways echo the message of the Gospel passage.

After the Gospel reading, Luke 15, the young priest, Tom, preaches from the pulpit (which is not raised) a sermon of about 15 minutes based closely on the text. He cuts a traditional figure in his vestments, but not a distant one; he clearly has a warm relationship with the people gathered, and makes references to a recent parish social evening and a forthcoming pilgrimage in which he will be sharing with a couple of dozen of his congregation. The sermon has the feel of devotional instruction; delivered clearly, with integrity but without great emotion, it is listened to quietly and with respect by the congregation. The message is straightforward, stressing God's readiness to forgive and accept the worst of sinners. By way of application in his Catholic context, he quotes the Pope's encouragement to the faithful to avail themselves of regular confession to a priest, repenting of their sins and receiving the assurance of forgiveness. But most importantly, he reminds them how in the eucharistic celebration they can experience the forgiving love of God afresh.

The main aim of preaching like this is to help the worshipper encounter God within the service of which it is a part. This reflects the tradition of 'liturgical preaching' mentioned in Chapter 1. This is the concept which lies behind regular preaching in not only the Roman Catholic Church (which has accorded considerably more importance to preaching since the Second Vatican Council), but many Anglican churches, though worshippers and preachers may not always realize it! (I grew up in the 1960s in an Anglican church where such preaching was the staple diet – and good and memorable it was too – but I don't think I encountered the *idea* of 'liturgical preaching' until the late 1990s![1])

This kind of preaching can claim New Testament origins. It is significant that the sermon at the opening of Jesus' ministry took place as part of a synagogue service (Luke 4.16-21). In the Early Church, the words of prophecy and revelation given within the Christian gathering reflected in 1 Corinthians 14 were clearly words through which the group's sense of God's presence and direction were enhanced – that is, words conditioned by their context of worship.

Such preaching is normally based on an interpretation of one or more of the Bible passages that have been read as a part of the liturgy of the day. (Bible readings, in this tradition, always have their own place 'as of right' in the liturgy, and are not just subsumed within the sermon; it is normal to follow an authorized lectionary in the choice of readings.) It will often have a devotional tone, aiming to enable the listener to enter fully into the worship, above all the celebration of Holy Communion. The worshipper is thus equipped to re-appropriate the grace of God in Christ that the sacrament mediates, and to respond with renewed dedication.

I believe that a great strength of such preaching is that it is self-consciously only one act in the drama, albeit a crucial one. It recognizes that the proclamation of the gospel is going to take place in many other ways too: in song, prayer, reading and sacramental action. Thus it does not try to take everything over. In the example given, it was significant that though the priest preached, he did so on a level with the people, and as part of a service in which others took an active part. This was 'their' event, not merely 'his'. This strength is maximized when careful attention is given to integrating the various elements of the service. This does not mean choosing hymns or songs which all say just the same thing – or labouring the message of the sermon in the prayers! – but orchestrating the event so as to allow the rich polyphony of the gospel to be heard. The fact that, compared to other types of preaching, this kind is often quite short, should be seen in this light. It stems from the recognition that God's word is made known by many means.

A significant determining factor of preaching is what the particular Church believes about entry into the family of God. In churches with a 'liturgical preaching' tradition, this entry is marked primarily in sacramental fashion, and spiritual regeneration (though seen as essential) is not seen as necessarily linked to a 'conversion experience'. Thus another key characteristic of such preaching emerges: it aims constantly to remind the baptized of the good news on which their Christian identity is based. In other words, the preacher in this tradition treats his or her hearers as being, in the main, 'part of the family', but needs to go on reminding them what that means. In the example above, the key point of application concerned the need for regular confession of sin.

This kind of preaching is not directly or primarily an act of 'mission' or 'education'. That is not to say, however, that such preaching is inappropriate for a church that is conscious of its need to engage in mission and education. Rather, it takes its place within the wider spectrum of the church's life. In contributing to the congregation's encounter with God in worship, it contributes to their weekly renewal for mission. It can also, for any visitors, offer an unselfconscious statement of some aspect of our Christian story, such as will whet the appetite for further enquiry. Educationally, it offers (as it were) a normative centre for a range of more informal activities and groups in which, ideally, all ages are encouraged at various times to grow in Christian understanding and discipleship. It is a 'category error' to accuse such preaching of failing to employ the most up-to-date educational methods if education is not its primary business.

Nonetheless, the question of whether in a decreasingly biblically literate environment, liturgical preaching *should* aim to adapt to fulfil more of an educational function should be taken seriously. If the Sunday service is the only church event of the week (or even the month) for many of the congregation, it is important to maximize the opportunity for Christian nurture. At the same time, trying to overload the content of any particular service is counter-productive. Perhaps more churches with a liturgical preaching tradition could consider adopting the common American model of an adult 'Sunday school' preceding or following the main act of worship. This maintains the integrity of the preaching event as primarily a moment for worshipful encounter, while allowing a ready opportunity for those who wish to dig deeper during the same church 'visit'.

It is, however, very clear how liturgical preaching is nevertheless intimately bound up with the pastoral care of the congregation. The preacher will normally be the parish priest, minister or some other authorized person with pastoral charge in that place. The application of the message will be deeply conditioned and suggested by his or her knowledge of and relationship with the regular hearers. This is a subtle matter and naturally the preacher will always want to avoid breaking confidences or 'pointing the finger'. The line between pastoral appropriateness and misusing the platform of preaching to drive forward a particular personal agenda for the church is sometimes a difficult one to tread. There is a parallel here between preaching and individual counselling: both need to strike the balance between deep attentiveness to the actual human situation and the readiness to address it with words which, while always caring, may not always be comfortable.

Example 2

A multicultural congregation of 700 or more, including many people in their 20s and 30s, packs an evangelical church in a provincial city centre for mid-morning worship. An earlier service has attracted more families, and children have had their own teaching session during that time. In the crowds, many people could have remained anonymous.

The service follows a printed order. Apart from some words of confession and offering, the only vocal participation expected of the congregation as a whole is the singing of five rousing hymns, one of which is a traditional favourite, the others modern. Members of the congregation lead prayers, do the only Bible reading (of the text to be preached on) and sing a solo. CCTV allows parents in the crèche to watch and listen too.

The service is led by two men in their 40s wearing suits and ties. Martin leads the worship, carefully introducing each part, and linking much of it to the sermon which is to come, clearly seen as the climax of the service. He also announces that tapes of the sermon would be available after the service. Daniel preaches.

The sermon is the last in a series on selected psalms. It is presented in a lively, vigorous manner and clearly structured on three points, based on three sections of the psalm, and focused on our need to find security in God rather than in beguiling 'idols' of today (two mobile phones are used as a brief visual aid, to illustrate the pressure to buy the latest gadgets). The congregation are urged to follow the text in the pew Bibles, and many do. Daniel's tone is serious, but warm and engaging; he respects the freedom of individuals to respond in an appropriate way.

The message is reinforced at various points that we are all sinners and can have hope of eternal life through Christ alone. Opportunity is offered at the end of the service for people to come to a designated space at the front for prayer for any needs.

This is an example of what is often known as 'expository preaching', a label used for a range of types of preaching familiar, especially, from evangelical churches. Such preaching is regularly at the *climax* of the service of worship, normally near the end. It is seen as the main point of the gathering and everything else that takes place seeks to enhance its message. 'Make sure I'm on by 11.15' is the kind of thing the expository preacher has been heard to say to the one who will be leading the worship: in other words, give me time to do justice to 'the word'.

Like liturgical preaching, expository preaching can claim to go back to the Early Church, in this case to its 'teaching' ministry especially.[2] Its fundamental impetus goes back, indeed, even earlier. It is based on the conviction that God's speech or revelation is absolutely primary. He has shown himself to us, and our faith is based not on ideas we have dreamed up ourselves, but on something we have received, that has imposed itself upon us. The corollary of this is that nothing should replace or diminish the primacy of the preaching of the word in the assembly of God's people. The word is not only to be spoken, it is also to be recognizably treated as more important than everything else. And 'the word' here is normally closely identified with Scripture – whether the sermon is based on a single text or a doctrine linked to various texts.

In modern times the impetus for this approach was given by the Reformation. One of the Reformers' central complaints was that the primacy of the word had been lost. The Church no longer had a sense that it was *under* authority. Its ministry had become so closely *identified* with the ministry of Christ that it had forgotten its need to place itself *under* that ministry. In practice this meant recovering the importance of Scripture – the standing, unchangeable testimony to apostolic teaching – and the importance of preaching – the means whereby the voice of the living God could be heard afresh in the Church. The two were intimately linked: the voice of the living God was to be heard precisely as the preacher unfolded afresh the truth of Scripture. This reminder from the Reformers that we are all under God's authority is one that we all need to go on hearing, however it may be expressed in our various practices of worship.

'Expository' preaching seeks above all to unfold or 'expound' the meaning and significance of Scripture. In Britain the greatest living exponent of expository preaching is John Stott, who offers this striking definition: 'The expositor prizes open what appears to be closed, makes plain what is obscure, unravels what is knotted and unfolds what is tightly packed.'[3] Such preaching may have a fairly loose, verse-by-verse structure, as in much of the preaching of the Early Church,[4] and the consecutive expositions of Calvin. Or it may be more tightly ordered in some way. Stott himself is well known for the logic and order of his sermon structures; the most well-known British twentieth-century practitioner of the verse-by-verse approach was Martyn Lloyd-Jones. Sermon series are often preached, which may give more scope for thorough exposition of biblical books than sermons tied to the lectionary. The life of expository sermons is frequently prolonged through their availability on tape and now also through the Internet.

A distinct form of preaching that may be brought under this heading is 'doctrinal' preaching, that is, preaching on a doctrine derived from Scripture rather than on a single text. This kind is included here because like 'expository' preaching generally, it is rooted in a belief in the primacy of the ministry of the word within public worship. Doctrinal preaching became popular in the post-Reformation period, particularly among the Puritans, though it had earlier antecedents. In an age of controversy it could be an important tool for the advancement of a particular movement such as Calvinism or Arminianism. It could be argued that there is an important place for such preaching today, when the riches of Christian theology are comparatively little tapped by many churchgoers; though preachers need to beware of peddling a divisive partisan approach which assumes the absolute rightness of their own brand of the faith. ('Liturgical' preaching tends to approach the great doctrines of the faith via the Church's calendar of days and seasons that recall them.[5])

In an example of expository preaching such as the one described, the preaching is much more directly an act of 'mission' than in the case of liturgical preaching. A large crowd, many of them quite anonymous, are given instruction and challenge that, it is hoped, will lead them to faith. The very size and anonymity of the setting may contribute to a sense of freedom and safety to respond, or not, to the message. Expository preaching also aims to be 'educational' – a good 'Bible teaching ministry' is what is sought by those advertising for a new minister in churches of this tradition. At its best, its clarity makes for memorability and effective pedagogy, though the temptation to prolong a message unduly and pack it with too much detail needs to be resisted.

In some settings the 'mission' and 'educational' aims of such preaching are in tension, which may be resolved by gearing different services to different hoped-for congregations, leading to a distinction between a 'teaching' sermon and an 'evangelistic' sermon. This distinction may be problematic, however, in an era in which the boundaries around many congregations are increasingly fluid and people react against being pigeonholed.

What this kind of preaching is less fitted for – at least in large settings like the example above – is the pastoral role. If you are preaching to a congregation of several hundred it's quite impossible to have a meaningful grasp of the needs and situations of all the hearers. Indeed, in such settings the hearers may scarcely constitute a stable 'congregation' at all. This does not mean that the preacher can simply ignore the hearers' perspectives and world views, and a keen awareness of cultural trends and undercurrents will give real bite to the exposition of Scripture, as happened in this case. It simply means that the real pastoral work of helping people engage with the implications of Scripture for their lives needs to (and often does) take place in smaller settings. Again, we see that sociological and ecclesiological factors set natural limits on the function of preaching.

Example 3

A congregation of about 70 gather for morning worship in a suburban church from one of the mainstream Free Church denominations. In addition to this number, a 'junior church' of about 25 children with teachers is present for the first 10 minutes of the service, which includes a short address on the theme of 'journeys'. This is given by the minister, Helen, who conducts the whole service. She wears a preaching gown.

The notice sheet invites people to use the time before the service begins to read through the Bible passages chosen. There are some pew Bibles available, though not at every seat. It also asks worshippers to stand as the Bible is brought in at the start of worship, because this particular branch of the Church 'recognizes God's word as its supreme authority'.

After the children leave, most of the rest of the service is taken up with the two Bible readings (read by members of the congregation) and the sermon. The minister, who conducts the whole service as well as preaching, is a regular visitor, in her 60s. The person who welcomed her at the start has already revealed, in an off-the-cuff comment about 'looking forward to her message', the central place of the sermon in this church's worship tradition.

The sermon takes perhaps 25 minutes of the 60-minute service. It includes discussion of the two Bible passages, the story of God's call to Abraham in Genesis 12 and Jesus' meeting with Nicodemus in John 3, but it is organized around the controlling theme of 'unexpected journeys'. It includes stories of the preacher's own journeyings, literal and metaphorical. The tone is reassuring, even soothing, and the presence of Christ in all our journeyings is emphasized.

The type of preaching represented here may best be labelled 'thematic', because its organizing principle is a theme rather than a text. It is distinguished from the 'doctrinal preaching' identified above because the 'theme' is broader than a specific doctrine. It may be a scriptural word or concept, or a topic of interest in the contemporary world. Although Helen's sermon came from a tradition that gives a high value to Scripture, and the sermon formed the most substantial part of the service, the Bible passages were not brought to the listeners' attention in their sharp detail or specificity. Nor was any Christian doctrine being expounded. The sermon was based on the general theme of 'unexpected journeys' that controlled the whole service. Such preaching is common in churches of a 'broad' or 'liberal' tradition, especially within Free Churches, in which the worship leader/preacher is not bound to a lectionary and may thus have more liberty to give a thematic stamp to the service as a whole.

Thematic preaching owes its basic rationale to biblical patterns. The prophets, for example, were not expositors! They aimed to bring a divine viewpoint to bear on the situation of their people and the surrounding nations. Their subject matter was wealth and poverty, war and peace, justice and wickedness. Jesus himself was a prophet of this kind. His parables focused on everyday life – not as mere 'illustration' for some spiritual truth, or explanation of a sacred text, but as a way of transforming people's perspective on everyday life itself. His shorter sayings often had a paradoxical, ironic twist like those of the sage or the wit, and have similarities with the 'wisdom' literature of the Old Testament, which comments not primarily on text or law, but on creation and human life. Something similar is seen in the apostles' preaching. In Acts 2, Luke recounts the first Christian sermon as being Peter's explanation for the strange event the crowds have just witnessed. In the process Peter expounds the significance of Joel 2.28-32 and Psalm 16.8-11, but the exposition serves the explanation of the event, not the other way round. Thus the 'preaching' of the prophets, Jesus and the apostles can all be seen as focused upon the world, shedding upon it the light of divine revelation.

This indeed set the basic orientation for the Church's preaching up to the Reformation, and is a perspective that preachers of all traditions should learn from. In the Early Church 'figural' interpretation was important: scriptural texts were interwoven with contemporary realities, so that the world could be seen in the light of God's truth. It was easy, however, for Scripture to become tamed and twisted in this process – hence the Reformation's emphasis on the importance of letting Scripture itself be heard with new clarity. Unfortunately, the preaching of post-Reformation Protestantism often descended into arid biblicism and partisan controversy, in which the vital connection between received truth and contemporary life was lost. The link was restored, with varying emphases, in the Pietist focus on the importance of Christian experience and the attempts of great liberal theologians such as Schleiermacher to re-establish the intellectual connection between faith and culture. In the twentieth century, Harry Emerson Fosdick in the USA and Leslie Weatherhead in the UK were influential preachers who grasped the need for a focus on this world and the human condition within it.

Although the distinction between 'expository' and 'thematic' preaching may look superficially like a theological one – the former 'evangelical', the latter 'liberal' – the more fundamental distinction is one of focus. Expository preaching *focuses* on Scripture, and then seeks to make applications of it to the contemporary world.

Thematic preaching *focuses* on the world, and then seeks to understand it in the light of Scripture. It is quite possible to approach either task from a background of either evangelical or liberal theology: so here is a good example of how a call to learn from different sermon types is not necessarily a call to change one's fundamental theological convictions (though one hopes that all preachers will be open to the fine-tuning or even changing of those convictions too, where necessary!)

As with 'liturgical' preaching, the missional and educational function of 'thematic' preaching like Helen's is indirect rather than direct. However, it is clearly well suited to the pastoral task. At its best, such preaching achieves a deep integration between the drama of life and the drama of Scripture, shedding shafts of light in both directions. The risk you perpetually run with thematic preaching is of obscuring the excitement and strangeness of the scriptural drama beneath a rather flattened version of the life drama that has been imposed upon it.

Example 4

A few miles away is an unassuming looking building, an old church hall which has been taken over by a new church fellowship in an inner-urban area. From some way away loud exuberant noises can be heard within. It is 12.30 p.m. on a Sunday; since before 10 a.m. smartly dressed men and women of all ages, nearly all black, have been here. Godwin, a wiry, fiery grey-haired man who is preaching, started his sermon about 15 minutes ago and has at least 25 minutes to go. He declaims – sometimes even shouts – his message with utter conviction into the microphone. It is about how the devil's temptations are turned into God-given trials. The congregation who fill the building respond enthusiastically with 'Amens' and 'Alleluias', in the same spirit in which they have been singing and praying since about 11 a.m. Before that, from 10 a.m., a small number of them have already gathered for an hour's detailed adult Bible class.

The small number of visitors feel very conspicuous, but are given a rousing welcome when asked to stand!

This event belongs in the tradition of 'revivalist' preaching, which aims above all else at the renewal of people's lives. Like expository and (to some extent) thematic preaching, it regularly dominates the services in which it takes place. Unlike them, however, it revolves not so much around the *objectivity* of God's revelation in the text and the world, as its *immediacy* – the sense that he is working and speaking by his Spirit now. There may also be a lively sense that God's voice may come through others apart from the preacher, which can give the sermon a more dynamic link to the rest of the worship. Paradoxically perhaps, in view of the emphasis on the Spirit, 'revivalist' preaching may also emphasize (more than the other kinds) the need and ability of the individual to make a 'decision' for Christ. It is widespread in some kinds of evangelical churches and is the norm particularly in many Pentecostal churches, like the one depicted here.

The origins of this kind of preaching, too, may be traced to the New Testament. Peter's sermon in Acts 2, closely linked as it is with the coming of the Spirit and its implications, can again be seen as a paradigm case. The early assemblies as portrayed in 1 Corinthians 14 also display a sense of the immediacy of the Spirit's speech. The context of such preaching within worship is vital. Unlike the context for liturgical preaching, though, this is worship conceived not primarily as a sacramental drama but as an arena for the Spirit's movement. The conscious participation of leaders and congregation in this movement may be seen in the 'overflow' of corporate worship into the sermon itself, as the congregation actively respond to the preaching and urge it forward.

'Revivalist' preaching today is the heir of various movements in the Church since the Reformation that have stressed the need for the Spirit's working to bring about not only the new birth of unbelievers, but a revived Christian life among professed believers. The post-Reformation centuries, marked by an increasingly arid orthodoxy among the official churches and an increasingly dechristianized, morally rootless society, offered fertile ground for the rise of Pietism. From this soil grew the revivalist preaching of Wesley and Whitefield in the UK in the eighteenth century, and of Finney and Moody in the USA in the nineteenth century. In their different ways, Methodism, the Keswick Convention, the Salvation Army, Pentecostalism and the charismatic movement have given further impetus to this type of preaching. The most well-known modern exemplar (though not quite in the Pentecostal style exemplified above) is Billy Graham in the USA. For whatever reason, there has not in recent times been any revivalist preacher of his stature in the UK.

'Revivalist' preaching can only properly be understood with reference to its view of its hearers. The key point at which it differs from classic expository preaching in its origins and ethos is the perception that it must often take place outside the walls of the institutional Church. This was graphically symbolized in the open-air preaching of Whitefield and Wesley, the 'camp'-style meetings of Finney and the crusades of Moody and Graham – and is still seen in the large out-of-church events in Britain today such as Spring Harvest and New Wine, or the meetings addressed by J. John in London in summer 2003. It was because the 'masses' were no longer coming to church in the eighteenth century that the message had to be taken to them. That remains the rationale for evangelistic campaigns involving large meetings for preaching in a neutral setting. In a similar way, large gatherings for Christians are seen as providing an opportunity for teaching, fellowship and stimulus to growth of a kind that is not normally available in the local church.

It is interesting to see the effect of this movement beyond the borders of the Church on the relationship between preaching and worship. In practice, an element of worship has often surrounded this kind of preaching, even when directly aimed at the unchurched. The style of Billy Graham's crusades became familiar to many in Britain following his first visit in 1954: the careful 'build-up' to the address consisting of musical items and prayers, and the carefully orchestrated time of response following, with music playing while those who wished to give their lives to Christ 'got up out of their seats', going forward as an act of commitment and to receive counselling. There is then, for many converts, the difficult transition into the worship of the local church, which may well be very different in style from the crusade meeting. Some churches, however, have sought in their regular worship to replicate these meetings. This was particularly evident in the 'frontier' churches founded through the ministry of Finney in the USA. But it is also seen, for instance, in the Salvation Army's services, with their regular opportunities for people to come forward to the 'mercy seat' to receive Christ – a throwback to the 'anxious bench' of Finney's time.[6]

Where this kind of preaching is the dominant one within a local church, the need for a personal response to Christ is continually kept to the fore. The transposition of the 'frontier' evangelistic situation into regular public worship might be seen as one factor in the rise of movements stressing the need for personal holiness or a 'second blessing' among professing Christians. This is because the message of personal transformation was transferred from a situation where many of the hearers were unconverted to one where most of them were converted. In such churches opportunity may frequently be offered on the same occasion for different kinds of response depending on the individual hearer's condition. This may include prayer for healing. Paradoxically, although it is based on the call to change, it tends to take place in church contexts where the proportion of the already 'changed' is at its highest.

The function of 'revivalist' preaching, then, is primarily missional, but there is also a deep ongoing pastoral concern that regular members should enjoy all the spiritual blessings available to them in Christ. Christian education happens elsewhere, in smaller groups: at least some of the congregation described were willing to give up their whole Sunday morning, to study together before the main worship service. The challenge if you are preaching in such a setting, perhaps, is to be realistic about who the hearers actually are, so that both mission and pastoral care can be more effective. There is a need to remember that making meaningful connections with the hearers is a matter of careful pastoral listening as well as the inspiration of the Spirit.

This example also illustrates how cultural, as well as ecclesiological, factors affect preaching. It is easy for white British Christians to assume that 'their' ways of preaching are the natural or normal ones, but that of course is just one of many assumptions that the welcome proximity of many cultures in one nation now challenges. There is a rich tradition of 'black preaching' with its own distinct cultural characteristics,[7] including an emphasis on the imagination and storytelling, which are not merely a reflection of a revivalist (or any other) church tradition. And this itself of course represents just one among the many cultures now jostling alongside each other in the UK (and by no means represents all black preachers!) A particular challenge for preachers in many places is how to be true to themselves and their own cultural preferences while reaching out beyond their comfort-zones to address a congregation in which many cultures find a home.

Example 5

It's 'all-age' worship on Mothering Sunday. The building is full of a congregation of around 180, including members of uniformed organizations on 'parade', and 'occasional' visitors. The under-5s are taken out after about 15 minutes; everyone else stays in for the remainder of the hour-long service. (Some of the older teenagers who regularly attend stay away altogether, not liking services which they perceive as being geared to younger children.)

The service is conducted in a lively, friendly and humorous manner from the stage at the front, by the senior minister, Eileen. She's a grandmotherly figure with a twinkle in her eye. Two activities especially prepare the way for the talk towards the end of the service. The first involves pictures of 'celebrity' mothers being put up on a screen (using a data projector). The 'odd one out' is 'Mother' Theresa of Calcutta, and this prepares for the widening of the notion of 'mother' that will be explored later. The second takes place in conjunction with the reading of Luke 2.41-52. A group of volunteer children is recruited to circle the church with party-blowers, to capture the festive atmosphere of those returning from the Bar-mitzvah celebrations at Jerusalem. A volunteer adult couple graphically acts out the discovery of Mary and Joseph that Jesus was lost and their subsequent search for him.

Eileen's talk, of about 12 minutes, is based on the reading. During its three sections the congregation is asked to do simple hand actions:

first hugging oneself, indicating a mother's love; second an 'open book' position, indicating a mother's teaching; third stretching out one's hands, indicating a mother's welcome. All three of these are related to the tasks of motherhood generally, as exemplified especially by Mary, to God's role as the supreme parent, and to the different ways we can all fulfil a 'mothering' role.

The children participate in two short periods of prayer. Before the end of the service they come to collect daffodils for their mothers and grandmothers and other women in the church.

The past 40 years have seen an increasing emphasis on the importance of all ages, including children, having opportunity to worship meaningfully together. Whether on a weekly or monthly basis, many churches hold services specifically designed for 'all ages', in which children (except maybe the very young) as well as adults are invited to participate throughout. Let's highlight some of the characteristics of this type of preaching by comparing it with the others we have discussed.

'All-age' preaching of this kind is like liturgical preaching in that it is planned as just one part of an entire event containing various significant 'acts'. In some such services, indeed, the 'talk' may constitute quite a small proportion of the whole; or it may be so interspersed through the whole that it is barely recognizable as a discrete entity. But there may also be a tendency for one *theme* to control everything, and indeed Eileen's sermon in the example above could also be called 'thematic preaching', though it also had some of the characteristics of 'expository preaching' in being earthed in a single Bible story.

'All-age' preaching also has similarities with 'revivalist' preaching, which, as we saw, tends to have a more dynamic and less formally demarcated blend with its surrounding worship context than the other kinds. However, it generally differs markedly from 'revivalist' preaching in its lack of intensity of appeal for response. This comes from its awareness of its listeners. There is a widespread understanding – cutting right across the varieties of ecclesiology, baptismal practice and the like – that the Church's task with its children is at least primarily to 'teach', to lay foundations, rather than to 'proclaim' or seek to 'convert'. This raises important questions about the place and ethos of children's missions and outreach activities, whether organized by a church or on a parachurch basis. Here we just note the recognition that the intensity of appeal for conversion or spiritual renewal, which has a place in adult worship contexts, is not appropriate in the same way when a significant number of children are present.

So maybe 'all-age' preaching is really a kind of expository or thematic preaching, with its emphasis on 'teaching', but transposed into a key that makes it accessible to children? Certainly the 'all-age' worship example above involved, essentially, a 'teaching' sermon helping listeners of different ages to reflect on the significance of the biblical story and the theme of motherhood. But this does not mean that we can or should ignore the real *spiritual* experience and needs of children, and 'all-age' preaching can equally be a variety of either liturgical or 'revivalist' preaching, aiming to facilitate an encounter with God. It is possible and desirable to deal with profound truth in addressing children, provided you do so in accessible language. Much anecdotal evidence suggests that adults listening can greatly benefit from such 'talks'. Even if you are not expecting a response in either sacramental or revivalist terms, children can be helped through the talk to participate meaningfully in the worship gathering and respond to God in a way that is right for their stage of growth. Carefully handled dialogue between preacher and listeners may be one way in which you can enable this to happen.[8]

This kind of 'preaching' marks a departure from the predominantly monologic nature of the preceding types (though in the sweep of history, this is not a novelty!) Interaction in an 'all-age' service is an explicit expression of an insight that has been increasingly applied to preaching more generally: *we are not simply trying to 'get something over', but to create a space and an opportunity for people of whatever age to encounter God and engage with his truth for themselves, on a variety of levels.*

Such preaching, then, can be a significant 'mission moment' in the life of the Church, especially on occasions such as Mothering Sunday when many non-regulars come. It is an opportunity to express the gospel in an attractive, accessible way that yet evokes a sense of wonder. In its concern for all ages and its readiness for interaction it can also fulfil a significant pastoral role. As the informal nature of the service allows for a variety of elements, it may be much more effective educationally than more traditional forms of preaching.

However, there are considerable challenges and risks involved here which should not be underestimated.[9] The gathering is sometimes 'sold', framed and conducted more as entertainment than as worship, thus not only rendering encounter with an awe-inspiring God more difficult, but also compromising its potential missionary character. Pastoral concern for some (usually the 8s to 13s and their parents) may exclude others (the teenagers, the single and the elderly, for instance). Or an educational thrust may so drive the whole occasion that it becomes more like a (perhaps chaotic!) version of school than an occasion of worship. It is possible to do 'all-age' worship and preaching well – as in the occasion I briefly described above. But these cautions underline the imperative of thinking very clearly what we are doing, and why, before jumping on a bandwagon or reaching for the latest off-the-peg templates.

Another type of preaching which is important to mention, though it may often not be within a setting of worship but in some more 'secular' setting such as a student debating forum, is apologetic preaching. Apologetics is the activity of defending the Christian faith, engaging seriously with objections to it and commending it on an intellectual level. This is surely a healthy thing for all preachers to be involved with at some point!

Apologetic preaching has an important function with respect to those who already have faith as well as those who do not. It strengthens the confidence of believers and equips them for giving an account of their hope when called on to do so (1 Peter 3.15). You don't need to be in an academic setting to engage in it; 'civic' churches and cathedrals, indeed any church with a prominent role in the community, offer an excellent base. One could argue that apologetics should be a core activity in such places! These churches may not only attract large numbers of spiritual seekers, as yet uncommitted, but also be a platform for well-known speakers, whose words may be reported more widely.

The antecedents of apologetic preaching are found first in the engagement of the Church Fathers in debate with opponents of Christianity, during the centuries when the Church needed to establish itself intellectually over against Judaism and paganism. In modern times, it can be traced back to the eighteenth-century 'age of reason', when Christians found themselves on the defensive in the face of a growing secularist outlook and philosophy. As an approach, it is not tied to a particular theological tradition. It is often associated with Evangelicalism. However, one of the great early practitioners (though this label may not have been given to him at the time) was the seventeenth-century Broad Church Anglican Archbishop, John Tillotson. And a distinguished contemporary apologetic preacher is Archbishop Rowan Williams, generally regarded as belonging within the 'Catholic' tradition of Anglicanism.[10] The content and style of apologetic preaching today is likely to be profoundly affected by the preacher's understanding of the 'postmodern' mindset and milieu, as well as sensitivity to the range of media which pervade contemporary life.

We believe there remains an important place for apologetics. The applicability of Christian faith to every area of cultural and intellectual life needs to be demonstrated still. However, the defensiveness which often characterized it in earlier generations – leading to Christians trying to persuade others of the validity of their faith using the very canons of secular reason which were the cause of objections to faith – needs to give way to a confident readiness simply to share our great Christian narrative on its own terms, and let it persuade people through its own attractiveness, grandeur and integrity.[11]

Identifying key types of preaching is not a way of trying to box preachers or congregations in. I've done it because I believe it is very important that the preacher reflects on the rationale and purpose for preaching in a particular setting, on a particular occasion. There are of course many creative combinations possible; but there are also perils in a mix-and-match approach. This is because the act of preaching *never belongs to the preacher alone; it is a social event involving a group of people*. A preacher who gives a lengthy exposition in a situation where a liturgical sermon is expected, or a revivalist rallying-call in a situation where some gentle 'all-age' teaching is called for – or, of course, vice versa – is (whether wittingly or unwittingly) breaking a social compact, with all the attendant risks. These are considerable, given the very public nature of preaching. Of course, there will be the odd occasion when an overturning of expectations is right, but in that case the preacher should understand clearly what he or she is doing. 'What should this sermon aim to do in this context?' is one of the most fundamental questions to be asked by the preacher beforehand.

All the types of preaching discussed here are well-established, and some readers may well be thinking that I have so far avoided facing the question of whether in the light of changing circumstances in Church and world, a radical overhaul may be needed of any or all of them. We shall indeed return to that question, especially in Chapter 10. But I hope to have shown in this chapter *both* that 'preaching' is not some monolithic phenomenon that can be lauded or knocked without reference to the actual variety of preaching events, *and* that the established types of preaching continue to have their own rich life, logic and potential.

For now, we turn from the *practice* of preaching to explore a *theology* of preaching which seeks to do justice to the mysterious, many-sided nature of these varicoloured events.

3

The players in preaching

Stephen Wright

Some readers might be thinking: so where is God in all this? We've looked at the variety of things that preaching might be doing in different contexts: evoking worship, expounding revelation, nurturing faith, inspiring renewal. But isn't there something more fundamental going on in all these contexts? Across the whole range of Christian traditions, there is a hope that somehow, in preaching, God himself will speak.

This is a liberating hope, not excusing the preacher from hard work, yet removing the strain and burden of thinking that the effectiveness of the event is all down to him or her. Yet the claim that God speaks in preaching is an awesome one, which needs to be carefully qualified. We may occasionally have heard preachers whose confidence that they were speaking 'the word of God' was tantamount to asserting infallibility. This can be a frightening and oppressive experience. Fortunately, few preachers would wish to go this far! But that just returns us to our question: where exactly is God in the event of preaching? How can we seek to let our words be a channel for his word, without either making overblown claims or despairing of our own frailty?

In this chapter we will explore a theology of preaching as an 'act' of five parties: God, the Church, Scripture, the congregation and – finally! – the preacher. We will see that such a theology is never a merely theoretical matter, but touches at every point on our actual habits and practices of preaching. The hope is to see the expectation that God will speak in its proper light, giving due weight to the other 'players' also.

An act of God

Put aside thoughts of 'an act of God' as some dreadful disaster! To see preaching as (in some sense) 'an act of God' is based on a wonderful conviction. The God who spoke through the prophets, through Jesus and through the apostles *continues to speak today*.

We sometimes forget that the same Reformers who returned the Bible to centre stage in the life of the Church had an equally high view of preaching itself. Remember the Second Helvetic Confession, quoted in the Prelude: 'The preaching of the Word of God *is* the Word of God'. Of course, this immediately raises huge questions. What counts as 'preaching'? Who is to decide what is, and is not, the 'word of God'? How can we protect ourselves against large numbers of megalomaniacs claiming to speak for God and wreaking all kinds of havoc and destruction in the process?

But before we rush to give answers to these questions, we should pause to let God be God. If he is indeed a God who shows himself and speaks to us, as we claim, there is a fundamental sense in which it is not up to us to predict and decide how or where or by whom he does or will do it. We should, rather, be ready for his word through whatever channel it may come.

In the last century Karl Barth called the Church back to faith in a God whose speech is truly free. Nothing we can do by way of argument, rhetoric, communication skills, even faith or spirituality, can *produce* the word of God. All we can do is *respond* to the word of God.[1] This means that we can never *guarantee* that God will speak through a sermon, or any other means – or that we can, as it were, capture and pre-package a message we have received from him, and pass it on so that others will receive it just as we have. He is free to speak as he wishes, through, between or even despite our words. Our part, as preachers and congregations, is to *listen* to what God has said in the past and *pray* for him to speak afresh today. We remember God's promises and place our trust in them. We look expectantly to what God will do now and in the future, knowing that this will be consistent with his unique self-revelation in Christ.

However, we need not fear that that word will come in conflicting and confusing ways which leave us wondering what is God's message and what comes from a human ego. For the same event which triggered the outpouring of the Spirit of prophecy on 'all flesh', allowing the word of God to be heard through all kinds of people and in all kinds of places (Acts 2.17,18) is the event to which God has for ever anchored his word. The Spirit did not fall on the disciples in such a way as to enable them to say whatever they wished. The Spirit came on them precisely so that they could bear witness to what they had seen and heard: to the life, death and resurrection of Jesus. So when anyone who purports to speak the word of God does not speak of what pertains to Jesus, or turns the apostolically proclaimed Jesus into a different Jesus (cf. 2 Corinthians 11.4), we know that their claim is false. There is thus a Trinitarian shape to Christian preaching. It is an act of God the Father, through the power of the Holy Spirit, which serves to illuminate God's Son, Jesus Christ, whom we know as 'the Word of God' (John 1.1-14).

But if God is free to speak thus at any time and place, what is the function of those 'set- piece' occasions that we call preaching? It's helpful to think of them as *representative* events. God doesn't necessarily speak to people more loudly or excitingly or freshly in preaching than he does through other means. But preaching acts as a 'reference-point' for all those other moments in which God may also reveal himself. Through pointing to Christ, preaching helps people to discern what is of God and what is not in all other events that might appear to reveal him. In this sense preaching is a *sacramental* act. Just as baptism and Holy Communion are not regarded by any Christian tradition as the *only* ways in which God draws near to us, but are rather *representative* ways, enabling us in symbol to take to heart again the central facts of Christ's dying and rising for us, so it is with preaching. It is not the *only* way in which God speaks to us, but it is a *representative* way, enabling us to focus on the heart of the gospel. The act of preaching is a pledge of God's continuing promise to us. In all our inadequacies as preachers and hearers, in these moments we seek to be open to the voice of God even though we can never predict or control it.

Thinking of the sermon in sacramental terms is liberating for the preacher. It is a reminder that God is speaking in various ways to various people all the time, and we are seeking to enter into that conversation. It is a reminder that we are caught up in a movement of God far greater than our own acts of preaching. Thus though it would be presumptuous to claim that every sermon is indeed 'an act of God', preaching itself is a *sign* of that action, of God's promise to speak to us. That is an encounter for which we can earnestly listen and pray every time we prepare either to preach or to hear a sermon.

An act of the Church

As a preacher I've often felt lonely. The whole process can seem so highly individualized – burying one's head in one's books, and seeking through prayer to hear what God would say. The message is born in secrecy and you, you alone, seem to be the judge of whether it's worth preaching.

But I wonder if there is a serious imbalance in this mindset, resulting no doubt from the individualism of the modern era. Is there a danger that we start wearing this loneliness as a badge of honour? Do we, indeed, find that moment when the secret is disclosed to the congregation the source of an illicit thrill – as if it was all about springing a wonderful surprise on them each week? The theological reality, surely, is that when we speak we do so not merely as individuals (though clearly the message must touch us personally). We do so as representatives of the universal Church. This, too, is liberating.

It means, for instance, that we are freed from the burden of having to offer merely private opinions, like newspaper columnists. Of course, we will have such opinions, and there is a time and a place to share them. But as representatives of *the Church*, it is *the Church*'s distinct and unique faith we are called on to proclaim. We are also freed from the need to aim for endless novelty. We are called to speak in fresh and engaging ways, but it is an old, old story we tell.

The main practical consequence of this is that we should be immersed in the Church's story. Primarily this means Scripture, and we shall devote a section to that below, for Scripture plays a unique part in the preaching event. But it also means the story of the Church down the ages and the wealth of its thinking and practice, for which we use the shorthand label 'tradition'.

'Tradition' has a bad press in some parts of the Church. It has picked up negative associations of stuffiness and 'dead wood'. But in fact 'tradition' is the very opposite of this. Rightly understood, it is the lifeblood of the Church, as of any organization. In the reproduction of biological life, one generation gives birth to the next. In the reproduction of cultural, social and intellectual life, one generation passes its treasures on to the next. The reproduction of faith, though of course dependent in a special sense on God himself, in a human sense is no different from this. 'One generation will commend your works to another; they will tell of your mighty acts' (Psalm 145.4 NIV).

Every Christian generation has had its special stories of God's working in human lives and communities. In constantly fresh ways, the good news is embodied. These stories from the past become an ever-increasing treasure store to give hope and concrete shape to our proclamation of the good news in the present. God's past surprises encourage us to look for his future ones. Of course, there are the cautionary tales too, of Christian life skewed badly out of shape. 'Tradition' is not just Francis of Assisi and Mother Theresa; it is also the Crusades and the Inquisition. So engagement with tradition is not a matter of basking smugly in past glory, but humbly, honestly and self-critically remembering the mercies of God.

Tradition is passed on by various means. These are often very informal, leaving no tangible record behind them. Above all they are the sharing of the life and love of Christ. But they also include the expressions of faith in art, literature (even books of sermons!) and music, in ritual and symbol. The architecture of our church buildings, the songs that we sing, the prayers that we pray, are all part of the living tradition that we inhabit and the springs from which our preaching may draw.

One of the key vehicles of tradition is, of course, preaching itself. The gospel message was spoken before it was written. And what we preach today has been influenced in countless ways not only by what has been passed on to us in written form, but by the 'oral tradition' that is preaching itself.

Awareness of standing in this stream of tradition is both exhilarating and humbling. It also has practical consequences. First, it prompts us to be self-critical about our own message. In what ways has it been influenced by tradition, including the preaching of the churches which have been 'home' to us? Such influence may be positive or negative, but it is important to be aware of it. Ways of speaking about Christian truth that are presented as 'biblical' are often shaped in profound ways by quite recent tradition. We may think, for instance, of the way in which language of the 'new birth' has been so heavily used in some parts of the Church in recent decades, and has become devalued in the process. Such words and phrases can all too easily become mantras that are repeated almost superstitiously, gradually losing all living connection with the truth they are supposed to represent.

Secondly, a sense of tradition should also open us up to the variety of expressions of Church life today. In the twenty-first century we are part of a fragmented Church whose various parts have preserved precious elements of insight into the gospel and Scripture, but are often tragically cut off from each other. Preachers can open up one part of the Church to the riches of others. This does not mean uncritical adoption of others' traditions any more than one should be uncritical of one's own. But openness to the wealth of tradition is necessary precisely if we are not to idolize any single tradition or set of traditions, and keep returning to the Christ revealed in Scripture as the source, reason and inspiration for our faith.

An aspect of tradition is *theology*, extended reflection on God's revelation. A Church without theology remains stuck in the past, in the grip of *dead* tradition, because theology is the endeavour to understand, appropriate and apply the truth we have received *for the present time and place*. The preacher is at the forefront of this endeavour. As preachers pay attention to the theologizing of others, they will note both dead-end alleyways to be avoided, and promising pathways as yet hardly explored. They will have their own thinking tested for its faithfulness to God's revelation. They will enter into living conversation about the application of Scripture to today, and make their own contribution to the theology of the future.

An act of Scripture

Most Christian preachers will affirm the central importance of Scripture as the basis for preaching, even though they express this in a wide variety of ways. Here we will try to show how preachers with a range of views on this subject may allow Scripture to play a positive and dynamic role in their preaching.

It may sound strange to call preaching 'an act of Scripture'. Scripture is a book; it does not act as a person does. Moreover, it is a closed collection. Preaching is not somehow an enlargement of Scripture; the very essence of the canon is that it is an agreed list of books for use in the public worship of the Church. It cannot be augmented without fundamentally altering the identity of the Church. Nevertheless, the words of Scripture can 'come to life' in preaching and exercise power over the hearers and indeed the preacher.

Scripture calls us back to the heart of our faith, to the revelation of God in his Son Jesus Christ. Some argue for an absolute kind of authority for Scripture that in practice is difficult to maintain, given that Scripture itself does not purport to be either a comprehensive textbook of knowledge or a law-code designed to regulate all of life. At the other extreme, others would evacuate it of all effective authority, just co-opting parts of it where convenient by way of support for a particular ecclesiastical or social agenda. More honest than both these extremes is an approach that allows Scripture to be *heard* on its own terms. This can be an event of extraordinary power.

The right use of Scripture is a challenging goal. We shall explore in more detail what this entails for preachers and congregations in the next chapter. At this point let's just emphasize the importance of allowing Scripture to be *heard* in preaching, not simply overlaid with explanation or replaced by summaries. A key skill is not to *over*-interpret. There is a fine balance to be struck here. On the one hand, if we believe that God speaks through the words of Scripture, we will be modest about preaching: sometimes, it may not even be necessary! It is all too easy to press Scripture into an over-tidy shape, whether for theological or communicational ends – many a three-point sermon comes to mind. Maybe it is worth making a point of aiming for a leaner style of preaching from time to time, with fewer of the preacher's words, which allows Scripture to speak with its own rhetorical force. On the other hand, if God is a living God, there is no need to fear preaching which is creative in its engagement with the Bible. This does not mean using a text as a springboard for meditation on some related theme, and then leaving the text itself far behind; rather, it means allowing the text to inspire our own communicative gifts on a deep level, so that the text's message is authentically yet freshly echoed. More about this in Chapter 6.

When preaching allows Scripture to be heard, it can be an exhilarating experience. In fact, the good news may be heard for the first time as good news, overcoming the widespread tacit assumption that Scripture is full of 'you musts'. When we hear it, instead, announcing joyful events, delighting in the beauties of creation and pronouncing blessings, what new freedom that can bring. In that context, the warnings and commands it does indeed contain are heard with a new sharpness, but also a new sense of how we can heed them.

An act of the congregation

At first sight, calling preaching 'an act of the congregation' may seem as strange as calling it 'an act of Scripture'. Obviously the idea of preaching assumes that there will be hearers; but are they not just that – hearers or passive recipients, rather than active initiators or executors of the event? Surely the preacher is called to address and challenge the congregation with a word from beyond, not simply act as a mouthpiece for them – a puppet, pulled by congregational strings? There are, however, three reasons why regarding preaching as an 'act of the congregation' is essential to a fully-rounded theology of preaching. These are bound up with the first three assertions that we have discussed: that preaching is an act of God, an act of the Church and an act of Scripture.

First, if preaching is an act of God, then on the human side it 'belongs' to congregation as much as preacher. If these minutes of speaking and listening are moments of attentiveness for the voice of God, that is indeed a congregational event: he is their God as much as he is the preacher's. On one level, this seems obvious, and preachers naturally assume it – as when praying beforehand that God will speak to all those who are present. But on a deeper level, it is easy to forget the implications of it. The 'sacrament' of preaching is not complete unless the hearers partake in faith. It is important that an atmosphere of expectation is actively fostered.

Moreover, the way in which the congregation hears the voice of God is bound to go beyond – although it will not erase – the voice of the preacher. The congregation bring their own experiences, perspectives and prejudices to the event. It is to and through those, most of them naturally hidden from the preacher's eye, that God's word is addressed. Preachers are not in control of the effect of their words. And some of the most enriching occasions in the life of a church can be those where the 'sacred conversation' of preaching is prolonged; where preacher and hearers together can share in listening to what is being heard by different people, and explore the consequences.

An Anglican Reader in the north-west of England, Janet Proctor, undertook, over several months, an exercise of 'listening to the listeners'.[2] She followed an idea described by Roger van Harn involving a daily diary.[3] A group of eight or so from the congregation record, over a set period, questions, problems and causes for thanksgiving from their daily lives, and ways in which they have sensed the help and direction of God – through reading Scripture, regular devotion, interaction with others, or in any way at all. They especially record responses to the regular preaching over this period, and ways in which it has engaged with their personal situations. The preacher meets regularly with the group and allows their diaries to inform the preparation for her next sermon. Janet testified to the way in which this deepened her relationship with the congregation and their sense of ownership of the event of preaching.

Secondly, if preaching is an act of the Church in a universal sense, it must also be an act of the local congregation. The preacher not only represents the faith of God's people through time and space. He or she also represents the faith of *these* people.[4] If an enquirer wished to find out what this particular Christian group stood for, they might naturally expect to find a succinct account in the regular preaching that took place among them.

Confusion would naturally arise here if the enquirer discovered that preacher and congregation were radically at odds. Thus as an act of witness, preaching should never have to stand on its own; it should be verbalizing what the community is embodying. The preacher acts as a representative of the local Christian community, and gives public expression to their faith and self-understanding. The congregation acts to bear witness to Christ through the whole of their life and worship, including the preaching. The sermon thus acts as a focal point for the church's evangelism, though it may well not be the main channel for it.

However, in practice there is normally a tension here. An aspect of representation is leadership, and preachers are in a *de facto* leadership role, whether or not they are the official priests, pastors or ministers of the church. And leadership means not only acting as the voice of a community, but also going ahead of it.

So there will be times when the preacher is called to summon the congregation back to an aspect of the universal Church's faith that it has forgotten. The preacher then becomes a representative of the universal to the local. However, the process can also take place the other way round. A local congregation may need to remind the wider Church of something *it* has forgotten. Radical, discussion-based preaching influenced by liberation theology in Latin America has done this in recent decades, reminding the Church of its calling to serve and empower the poor.[5] Here the preacher becomes the representative of the local to the universal.

Third, if preaching is an act of *Scripture*, it must also be an act of the congregation, for Scripture belongs not only to the preacher but to God's people as a whole. One of the great achievements of the Reformation was to restore the Scriptures to the Christian world at large through translation into the vernacular. The notion that only a privileged few should have access to the written records of God's revelation was blown apart. As Scripture's voice is heard again in preaching, the congregation as a whole gather round and listen – the preacher as one of their number.

Preaching as a genuine congregational act is threatened by authoritarian preachers claiming direct personal inspiration, by an overly academic approach in which scholarship acts as a barrier to universal encounter with God rather than a gateway to it, or when the preacher is seen as merely the mouthpiece of an authoritarian Church. A response to such dangers, taken by groups such as the Anabaptists and Brethren, is to de-emphasize the role of the trained and/or ordained preacher. Congregations either meet around the Bible in settings where everyone can contribute, or are led in preaching by a variety of church members who may be recognized as 'elders' but beyond that have no official authorization and, often, no training. The risk here is that the danger of over-dependence on personal inspiration is multiplied. Congregations may be held in thrall to a dominant leader, fall out over different interpretations from (apparently) equally 'inspired' people, or become cut off from the wealth of mainstream Christian tradition. So is there a more adequate model for preaching which takes the congregation's relationship with Scripture seriously while guarding against these various risks?

The clue must surely lie in a theology of the body of Christ that takes the different gifts of the members seriously. If we accept Paul's teaching about these gifts (Romans 12.4-8; 1 Corinthians 12.27-31; Ephesians 4.7-13), we will recognize that there is a place for the authorized and gifted minister of the word, as well as an affirmation of the liberality of God in bestowing his gifts freely on the various members of Christ's body. But, by the same token, we will allow and affirm the place of the whole congregation in the discernment of the will of God and the interpretation of his word.

An act of the preacher

I have deliberately left the part played by the preacher himself or herself till last. It is only when this part is seen in the context of all the others that we will be able to gain a focused vision of our task.

I have already suggested various implications for the preacher arising from preaching's being an act of God, the Church, Scripture and the congregation. The preacher is called to be one who is attuned to the voice of God, at home in the tradition of the Church, competent in handling Scripture and involved with the local congregation in the ongoing discernment of God's will. The authors of this book sometimes use the term 'representative' to describe this role. The act of preaching, and the human being who performs it, *represent* God, the universal Church, Scripture and the congregation.

How might we define this role more precisely? There is an array of conceptions on offer, and metaphors can illuminate the task, as long as they are not pressed too far.

In the *Church Times* interview for 2 November 2007, the former professional footballer Gavin Peacock, now an ordinand, compares the preacher to the football commentator: 'You have to be clear and concise.'

Yes, indeed – but we could probably think of some aspects of (even good) football commentary *not* to be emulated by the preacher! More familiar labels would be encourager, exhorter, evangelist, enabler, teacher, inspirer, disturber, prophet, herald, storyteller: the preacher may at various times (and sometimes all at once!) be all of these, and more. Some preachers, of course, will be more naturally gifted in one function than another. Some preaching settings, likewise, will call for one emphasis more than another. There is little point in trying to rank such functions. But is there perhaps one definition of the role that goes deeper than the others, which somehow undergirds them all – without which all of them would find themselves on shaky ground?

Thomas G. Long in his book *The Witness of Preaching*[6] identified the role of 'witness' as central and fundamental. We would support this analysis. It sharply expresses the representative function of the preacher.

Greatly simplifying Long's rich analysis of this idea, 'witness' captures the two sides of what the preacher is doing. On the one side, the preacher is pointing to truth *outside of himself or herself*. They are not claiming to be passing on ideas or visions that have simply occurred in their own minds. They are testifying to truth that has an objective quality: bearing witness to what God has done in history and is doing today.

But on the other side, the preacher points to truth *that he or she has apprehended*. We speak of objective truth, but we can only do so because we have subjectively perceived and latched on to it. In the famous words of Phillips Brooks, which we'll consider further in the next chapter, truth is mediated in the preacher through personality.[7] As representatives, we are concerned with the truth we are representing, but we will only be effective if we have to some extent internalized it.

To affirm the role of the preacher as witness is in fact to strike at the heart of some of the profound suspicion to which the public communication of faith has recently been subject.

On the one hand, both authors of this book accept the widespread verdict of recent philosophy that there is no such thing as a neutral, detached vantage-point from which to perceive truth. This is a verdict that the Church has always shared, and is indeed central to the biblical view of knowledge, wisdom and understanding (closely parallel ideas in Hebrew): the fear of the Lord is the beginning of wisdom (Psalm 111.10) and of knowledge (Proverbs 1.7). Thus the preacher can never claim to be a mere detached reporter: there is no such thing, and especially not where ultimate truth is at issue.

On the other hand, we are denying the verdict of some more radical recent philosophy that objective truth, if it exists at all, is quite unattainable, and that all claims to speak of it should be treated with radical suspicion. We believe that God *has* shown himself and that, fallible though we undoubtedly are, he enables us to speak truthfully of himself, though never of course to comprehend him.

What are some of the consequences for the preacher of this two-sided role of 'witness'? First, the 'objective' side calls for diligence in listening and learning and faithfulness in speech. If, as communicators, we are fairly to represent truth, we must open ourselves to it all the time, and seek to convey it honestly and courageously. Second, the 'subjective' side calls for self-awareness and self-involvement. We reflect on the impact of truth upon our own lives and allow that to be made visible in appropriate ways. What does it mean *for us* that (say) God is king, or that Jesus suffered, or that 'all things work together for good for those who love God' (Romans 8.28)? This 'subjective' aspect of being a witness entails a willingness to examine honestly our own responses to that of which we speak, to note the personal factors which might draw us deeply to some aspects of God's revelation while making others more difficult to relate to.

But does the idea of the preacher as 'witness' adequately convey the fact that preaching is meant to have an *effect*? At first glance it might seem too focused on the notion of just passing on information, whereas preaching at its best can have a powerful *transformative* function. This can happen directly or indirectly, within the Church's worship, mission, education and pastoral care.

In response to this, it is worth considering the following.

The nature of the truth to which we bear witness is such that it never leaves unchanged those who open themselves to it. On one level, this is so of all 'truth', even minor kinds. We are changed in small and subtle ways by what we see and hear each day. When we bear witness to those things, others are changed too. But it is, of course, especially true of God's revelation of himself. As we have seen, we cannot be genuinely open to this and remain unchanged at a deep level. And when we then bear witness to it in preaching, it will be life-changing for others. The act of Christian witness is never just a reporting of information. We find ourselves caught up – perhaps despite ourselves – into the role of advocates, even persuaders. As witnesses we want our words to *do* something, not just to *say* something.

Also, the power of the act of preaching does not lie just with the preacher. The preacher is only one of the players in the drama. The act of preaching has weight and effect in so far as it is not only an act of the preacher, but also of the Church, Scripture, the congregation and, above all, God himself. We are indeed caught up with advocacy, but the impact of the whole event is not ultimately dependent on our rhetorical skills. What it *does*, in the end, is out of our hands.

Finally, the beauty of the word 'witness' is that it reminds us of the simplicity of the task. We are to tell of what God has done. We are to share what we have seen and heard. There is an element of persuasion even in that, but it is God and he alone who will make our words effective for those who hear. This is no excuse for lack of care in choosing what to say and how to say it, but excellent warrant for not trying to predict or over-manage the outcome.

Bringing the players together

How then, in practice, can these five players be allowed their proper role in the event of preaching?

Our exploration thus far has been only the beginning of a theology of preaching. We must leave you to pursue for yourself, if you're interested, the ways in which various theological schools configure the players in the drama differently. The rest of this book explores the practical outworking of allowing these players their place, in the various processes surrounding the event of preaching: the preacher's own spirituality and embodiment of God's word; interpreting Scripture; preparing a message; sermon delivery; congregations and preachers working together to hear and proclaim the word.

4

The human preacher

Geoffrey Stevenson

> Preaching is the bringing of truth through personality . . . It must come
> through his (*sic*) character, his affections, his whole intellectual and moral
> being.[1]

The centrality of the person of the preacher in our enterprise cannot be evaded or denied. These words of Phillips Brooks (1835–93), Rector of Trinity Church, Boston, Massachusetts for over 20 years, provided a definition of preaching that is quoted perhaps more often than any other. So many other activities central to our society, from mathematics to plumbing to flower arranging, may be done without essential regard to the ethical and religious makeup of the practitioner. It can never be so with preaching, for a congregation will invariably discern where there is a mismatch between the character of the preacher and the truth of what is being preached.

In this chapter we are going to look at the personal qualities of the preacher, the task of lifelong development that this represents, and finally the place of honesty and self-disclosure in the sermon.

Personal qualities

So much has been written about the spiritual side of preaching, that an under-confident preacher may easily be discouraged. The responsibility for presenting the word of God to an expectant congregation weighs very heavily on some souls. A chapter such as this, speaking of the preacher's spiritual journey and walk with God, may induce further guilt with seemingly impossible ideals and exhortation to daily disciplines unsustainable in the rush of demanding ministry.

How tempting it would be to take the pressure off and adopt a theology of revelation that removes nearly all the responsibility for the power of God's word from the fallen and sinful preacher. Another equally appealing dodge might be to run towards so-called 'reception' theories of communication that stress the autonomy of the listener in making meaning from the sermon event. But there is no respectable theology of preaching that lets the preacher off the hook in this way.

Many writers on preaching have described – or prescribed – the essential components of the preacher's character. Quoting Brooks again, the required qualities merely to *begin* to make a preacher were: personal piety, unselfishness, hopefulness, good health, and a fifth 'intangible' centring on inspiration and inner enthusiasm. To these he adds that a successful preacher would almost certainly demonstrate the following 'elements of personal power': character, freedom from self-consciousness, respect for the people, enjoyment of the work, gravity and courage.[2]

This is a daunting list, but it is one that resonates with me. It is down-to-earth and realistic about the demands of preaching. I am sure you will have seen preaching ministries dragged down by ill-health or nipped in the bud by self-consciousness. The list calls as well for noble character traits that are often ignored by anodyne self-help or individualistic self-fulfilment programmes of secular society. These are qualities that speak of a life given to God for service and a daily taking up of the cross.

Fred Craddock wrote that 'the preacher is expected to be a person of faith, passion, authority and grace'.[3] I love the succinctness and the *sine qua non* quality of this list. Again, here are qualities of character, largely impossible to fake or to adopt superficially, but forged in the fires of experience and so much a work of God in the preacher's life.

'Postmodern hearers seem to value authenticity and vulnerability.'[4] Helpful words from Michael Quicke, British-born Baptist minister and now the Charles W. Koller Professor of Preaching at Northern Baptist Seminary in Chicago. Authenticity, as I understand it, is mostly achieved by experience, reflection upon experience, and sometimes scholarship (as in, 'She knows what she's talking about'), and it earns the preacher the right to be heard. Vulnerability implies humility as well as openness to change and even to being proved wrong.

Perhaps there is something more to vulnerability, though: Is it evidence of suffering, of having been through some of the same kinds of difficult experiences as your hearers? According to Ron Boyd-Macmillan, one of the four primary questions that a listener unconsciously asks of a preacher in the first five minutes of a talk is, 'Is the preacher wounded?' As he says, 'if brokenness doesn't come across, then the gospel doesn't come across'.[5]

Some years ago, there was a missionary who had endured years of hard and harsh service in the cause of the gospel in China, including imprisonment and torture. He came to speak at a conference of Western ministers and theologians. The subject of his brief address was the person and power of Jesus, and it was delivered in halting and sometimes hard-to-follow speech. This was not surprising considering the punishment his body had borne. Afterwards I overheard one minister remarking to another, 'He didn't say very much, did he?' His companion, more deeply moved, replied, 'A man hanging on a cross doesn't have to say anything at all.'

Vulnerability in a speaker is often more than evident without specific references or self-disclosure.[6] Listeners can sense and feel it. Classical rhetoricians recognized that a speaker's integrity has a huge role to play in the communication of the message, and for a Christian speaker modelling vulnerability is an inescapable part of being a witness to a crucified Lord who called his followers to walk the same path.

None of this is to deny or limit the action or sovereignty of God in the sermon. The trouble with 'truth through personality' as a definition of preaching is that it can have this effect if it does not recognize the authority and power of the Holy Spirit to bind together truth and personality.[7] Thus Robert Murray McCheyne is said to have written: 'The greatest need of the congregation is my personal holiness.' This is, of course, a work of God, who alone is 'changing us from one degree of glory into another'. Preparing to preach is not so much a lifetime's work, as a lifetime's grace. For our part, however, we still ask, how can the person of the preacher be grown, developed, nourished?

The lifelong development of a preacher

This cannot be entirely separated from the preparation of the preacher for a particular sermon, see Chapter 6, or indeed from the matter of the delivery of sermons, which we look at in Chapters 7 and 8. But here I want to move on to discuss some more general areas of the preacher's life:

- motivation to preach

- preparing to hear from God

- loving the listener[8]

- understanding communication, and

- understanding the cultural environment in which sermons must be preached.

The motivation to preach: *Tending the Fire*

Beyond a certain age, few people expect to be fired with enthusiasm for all of their tasks all of the time, whether those tasks are unseen service or exalted and honoured ministerial callings. Calling on God to cushion one from the tiredness and the defeats, in order to surf a wave of passionate ministry, marks a Christian who has not lived very long or a preacher who may burn brightly but be unable to sympathize with 95 per cent of his listeners. At the other end of the Christian life there is, of course, great danger when nothing surprises any more, for all is familiar. Seen it all before. Using the T-shirt to clean my car. Routine and discipline (having no doubt proved their worth in dry and difficult times) are recommended, but they do tend to dampen expectation of the exciting and unfamiliar. One may ask, is it realistic or even desirable to seek the wild, naïve enthusiasms of youth? But enthusiasm, a word which has only relatively recently left its etymological roots of religious zeal, *must* be woven into the process of preparation and delivery of a message that is about renewal, regeneration, hope for the future and the rebuilding of shattered and broken lives.

Furthermore, passion and fire in preaching may well be *inner* energies and not necessarily part of the delivery or the outer energy shown by the preacher. The latter will vary from personality to personality, more even than the difference between youth and old age. An inner passion, even to Jeremiah's 'fire shut up in my bones' is best not displayed in vocal histrionics and extravagant gestures – not in the British or northern European preacher, anyway. But there is scarcely a listener or congregation unable to tell the difference between one motivated by such passion and one who lacks it or is working from a sermon text that is not true to the preacher's life and experience.

Ron Boyd-Macmillan says that another of the four primary questions that a listener asks of a preacher in the first five minutes of a talk is, 'Is the preacher *alive*?' If so, they will have a passion that is strangely both convincing and attractive.

> There is the (possibly apocryphal) story about the pre-eminent philosopher and sceptic David Hume. One day a friend met him as he hurried along a road in London. 'Can't stop,' said Hume, 'I'm off to hear George Whitefield preach.' His friend remarked, 'Surely you do not believe what Whitefield is preaching, do you?' 'No,' replied Hume, 'but Whitefield does.'

David Day suggests:

> It is worth asking myself, what it is about God, Christ and the Christian life which gives me a buzz, excites me or stirs me inside. Where does my personal theology, no doubt impeccably orthodox, come alive, where does it spark and fizz? . . . Search for the points at which the spark arcs across the gap between the creed and your heart and let that truth set you on fire. Put bluntly, does anything about God excite you, or has everything gone stale and tired?[9]

The answer to those questions is, of course, at the crux of the preacher's identity and call. If your answers reveal a sickness or a lack, then the remedy lies at the core of the Christian religious tradition where you belong (though it is not unknown for God to break through to a believer from other, unfamiliar traditions). It surely involves seeking the face and presence of God, looking for an encounter with his living Word through his written word. Building on that, here are some of the popular and useful recommendations for preachers in need of the presence and inspiration of God:

- Read the sermons of the greats: Chrysostom (The 'Golden Mouth'), George Whitefield, Spurgeon, Sangster, Bonhoeffer, Martin Luther King, Martin Lloyd Jones.

- Listen to good contemporary sermons that can be easily obtained on DVD or web sites such as YouTube™.

- Read the biographies of saints – both in our times and in ages past.

- Consider the congregation and the people you serve in your preaching, the needs and the joys that they have. What is the consolation and inspiration that God may be wanting to bring them, perhaps only through you?

- Seek the company of a mentor / spiritual director / elder / confessor to share and pray with that person.

   Examine your heart and your conscience, to consider what might be blocking or dimming your vision of God. There's the well-known story of the Pentecostal minister asking an older minister how to pray for revival in his church. The older man said, 'Kneel down in your church, draw a circle around you where you are kneeling, and pray: "Lord, send revival within this circle!" '

- Finally, get in the habit of working with the Scriptures – and not just those that you are to preach on – asking questions persistently of them (and of God) until an answer comes. (On persistence in prayer, look up sermons of the great preachers on the parable of the Widow and the Judge in Luke 18.) Study and pray until there is an ember however faint that may be fanned into flame. Argue in your journal and even out loud with the commentators and other writers on the passages. You are interrogating the text, but Scripture, if we believe it to contain the word of God, must be allowed to interrogate you. Like Jacob wrestling at the ford of Jabbok, it may be painful, take all night and consume all the strength we have, but no one who wrestles in this way will be left unchanged. To then walk, limping, into the sunrise may be the part of the journey you must take to be the preacher that God has called you to be.

Stephen responds: 'I find the picture of wrestling Jacob a very powerful image for the deeply personal process of preaching. It suggests the lifelong and sometimes painful drama of being fashioned into the person, and spokesperson, God wants me to be. And yet this is one of those Christian paradoxes. On one level, I think the task of preaching is a human task like any other. That means that it has an end. The preacher, too, has a "sabbath". To forget that is to court idolizing our own labours. Conversely, being aware that preaching is a finite task, like all our other tasks, gives me the strength to carry it out. In a workaholic culture, the preparing of sermons can all too easily become just another layer in the blanket of stress which weighs upon us and dampens our spirits; and I don't think it's helpful to spiritualize this as if it is a matter of "wrestling with God". Anxiety and worry need to be named for the negative, dehumanizing forces they are.

Earlier in my preaching ministry I recall being quite paralysed on occasions when I seemed to have no message up until what I thought was a dangerously short time before I needed to speak! I think this showed a misconception of what waiting on God is about, and a lack of trust in the objective gospel which is always there, no matter how you feel, no matter how lacking in fresh ideas for presenting it you may be. Use an old sermon if you have to; even use someone else's, from the Internet or elsewhere, if you're really stuck; your own creativity is a wonderful gift, but don't get hung up if the creative spark seems to depart from time to time. It's a fallacy of modern individualism to think that preaching is all "down to you"; a fallacy of the "now" culture to think that preaching has to be super-fresh all the time.

Over the years I have come to value the pattern of "signing off" a Sunday sermon by Friday teatime at the latest. I then look over it quietly for half an hour or so on Saturday evening. Frankly, I have never stayed up all night to prepare and barring extraordinary circumstances, never intend to! Believing that God "gives sleep to his beloved", I find that it is far preferable to come to church in a relaxed frame of mind than with brow furrowed from creative or quasi-spiritual angst. Of course, I will always be dissatisfied with where I left my sermon on Friday night, even on Saturday night. Conscientious preachers will always feel that every sermon needs weeks or months rather than days to prepare properly! But it is far more likely that I will be alert to God and my hearers, and able to give

of myself with joy, if I come to the service refreshed, knowing that I
have done my finite task as well as I was able, with the strength that
God supplied, than if I am still uptight about whether it is "right" yet.'

Preparing to hear from God: *proceeding from silence*

Not exactly a personal quality or character trait, the words 'stillness' and 'silence'
speak of a tendency or personal strategy to seek and to spend time in places of true
spiritual nourishment and direction. These places may be physical, and of course
traditionally the desert has been a place to retreat to from the noise and busyness
of life. More accessible is the church or chapel, the garden, park or countryside
walk. However, stillness and silence can refer to psychological space, when a
slowing down, a letting go, a quenching of the chatter and the mental static can
give God space to be, not so much heard, as *encountered*. Such encounters,
mystics attest, are not generally speaking wordy affairs. Whether overtaken by awe
or wonder or ecstatic devotion, the individual granted a sliver of a fragment of a
tiny glimpse of God is not generally given to much speech. Nor does God seem to
do much talking either, however great the devotee's need to put the experience
into words. In the silence there is, as the Jewish mystic Martin Buber expressed it,
only 'I' and 'Thou'. Of course, such an encounter may not be commanded or
summoned; on the contrary, utter dependence on the complete sovereignty of
God's self-disclosure leads so often to mute adoration.

The silence in an encounter with God may also, often, be worryingly, devastatingly
empty. Indeed the 'silence of the absence' may in fact be the characteristic of God
that is least welcome but most formative of preachers and of those who would
choose to live their lives as friend and servant of the servant-preacher Jesus. Author,
Episcopal priest and preacher Barbara Brown Taylor wrote powerfully of the pain
and yet the presence of God most real 'when God is silent'. Reminding the reader
of Abraham and Isaac on Mount Moriah, Job's suffering, and much Jewish literature
after the Holocaust, she states:

> Only an idol always answers. The God who keeps silence, even when God's
> own flesh and blood is begging for a word, is the God beyond anyone's
> control. An answer will come, but not until the silence is complete. And
> even then, the answer will be given in silence. With the cross and the empty
> tomb, God has provided us with two events that defy all our efforts to
> domesticate them. Before them . . . our most eloquent words turn to dust.[10]

This is an inconvenient and bothersome thing to remember when as a preacher
what I most want to do is come up with some words, and quickly, that will keep the
congregation attentive for 10, 20 or 40 minutes next Sunday. Commentaries,
conversations, websites for sermons and sermon illustration are endless sources of

words and they seductively promise to come to my aid. But if I succumb to them too soon in the sermon preparation process, I may miss something vital. I may miss being shaped by God for my ministry, and this is fatal for the sermon.

Silence is not just a place where God is heard, giving a word to the preacher passed on in the next sermon. Silence – withdrawal – retreat – from the clamour of everyday life and from the busyness of Christian service is where many ministers encounter God most formatively and most fundamentally.

This takes time – and possibly the most challenging discipline is claiming and recovering time in which God can speak to us and form us. Time, as almost anyone in busy and demanding ministry knows, is eaten up by the urgent and pressing. If your personality drives you, as mine does, to seek the satisfaction of having measurable achievements at the end of a morning, or a day, then time spent in silence, time that is not demonstrably productive, will be often squeezed out in favour of, say, the suddenly terrifically important task of tidying and cleaning the kitchen, or giving the back gate a coat of paint . . .

More wisdom from Fred Craddock:

> . . . a preacher can recover and reclaim the silence that he or she carries within, and out of that silence, speak the Word. It demands the realization that a minister's life does not consist in the abundance of words spoken. But most of all it requires embracing both silence and revelation in one's understanding of God, and developing a mode of preaching which honours that understanding by being in harmony with it.[11]

Loving the listener: *till death us do part?*

To preach God's word is to share in a tiny way the unimaginable extent of God's involvement with, and love and compassion for all of humanity. Pain at the pain of another, grief for untimely loss, anger at injustice and unfairness, joy in the well-ness, the restorations and the reunions of individual and community: all are part of what it means to love the congregation being served pastorally. Of course, such love is costly, but it is vital for sermons that connect, and for this reason the offices of pastor and preacher have traditionally co-existed in the individual called to be a presbyter/leader. Writer and preacher Calvin Miller sums this up in his depiction of the preacher as *shepherd*. The shepherd or pastor guards, heals, tends and feeds the congregation – homiletically speaking. The pastor also *knows* the congregation:

> We can only preach to them – really preach to them – if we know who they are, the burdens they carry, where they work, and the heaviness of life that has gathered about them.[12]

In *Open Secrets*, Richard Lischer gives a powerful and moving account of his experiences as pastor of a little Lutheran church in the tiny town of New Cana, in rural Illinois. He freely admits that, after advanced theological work in Princeton and London, such a pastorate was not exactly in his career plan. But he preached and he prayed, fought and bled, laughed and loved and wept with people who were as needy and as saintly and as maddening as people are in churches anywhere. By the end of his time he had been touched and changed by God more, he thought, than the community to whom he was supposed to be ministering.[13] It is a rich and funny testimony of God shaping both a compassionate pastor and a blessed community out of what might have seemed to some as less than promising material.

For this kind of involvement and identification, I would suggest that both prayer and practical steps are needed. Books specifically written on pastoral leadership and Christian ministry (I can particularly commend John Pritchard's recent *The Life and Work of a Priest*[14]) are valuable here.[15] I know a minister working in a capital city and whose church has grown and provided a powerful ministry to a tremendous cross-section of society, from civil servants to artists and musicians to former drug-dealers. My friend preaches a faithful gospel message of hope and the presence of Jesus Christ, but he is not a 'great preacher' whom you would travel miles to hear. The worship, while contemporary and lively, is usually sung by a congregation who are pretty down to earth rather than 'lost in wonder, love and praise' the whole service. What makes the church such a beacon in the area is the community that has been formed, and most people there say that community is created and modelled in the minister's own household. The pastor and his wife often host huge Sunday lunches, their tiny apartment crammed (in addition to them and their four children) with the invited and the unexpected. Week in and week out, frequently at great cost personally and financially, my friend and his wife would open their doors to people in the church, offering hospitality and 'table fellowship', and sharing their lives where it made a difference to others. Did I say he was not a great preacher? Yes, but such involvement with the lives of his congregation certainly made his preaching great.

Your pastor's heart will grow (and occasionally shrink) with the joys and pains of the people you serve. Praying for them as well as you know them is one of the surest ways to resurrect patience, vision, hopefulness and a belief in the transformative and redemptive power of God. Getting involved, answering calls of distress, laughing over meals, crying over loss, hurting and being hurt, forgiving and being forgiven: these are the practical ways in which a pastor's heart is prepared for preaching.

Understanding communication: *tellers, guides and imagers*

Story and image (by which I mean not just art, icons and PowerPoint™, but metaphor, simile and example – in fact, pictures painted with words) are more enthusiastically received, and generate far longer attention spans than lists of facts and a barrage of reasons. But more fundamentally, story and image contain and convey truth of a far more profound nature than propositional truth. They are able to contain and convey truths such as the truth of knowing another person and being known by them. They can express and enshrine moral truth, and the truths known by a nation or community that shape their self-identity.

This view of truth exceeds concepts of 'mere' historical truth and factual accuracy. It does not deny such concepts, but it asks for some breathing room to be given to ideas of truth that have been dismissed by overly rationalist and scientific mindsets as romantic, or ephemeral or impossible to control and quantify, and therefore not useful. The Bible comes to us with *story* as its principal form, and with an overarching story or 'meta-narrative' that speaks of God's actions, of purposeful beginnings and intentional endings. Some philosophical theologians have pointed out that life is lived narratively, that is to say we experience and interpret our lives in storied ways, with a sense of beginnings and endings, of plot, character, complication and resolution. This means that meaning and identity are constructed at fundamental levels through narrative: through stories shared by communities, through stories told and retold between individuals, and through story rehearsed as inner dialogue as a way of building and buttressing the sense of self. Story, some say, 'goes all the way down'. Recognizing this in sermons means more than common-sense rhetorical techniques and the frantic Saturday search for an illustration to pad out an unconvincing point. Even sermons that are didactic contain exhortation and suggest practical application can be structured narratively (see the work of Eugene Lowry[16] and also Richard Eslinger's excellent chapter on narrative in *The Web of Preaching*[17]).

One drawback of being 'people of the book' is that we privilege and practise one particular mode of communication over others. I don't mean words over music or image. I mean *reading* over *telling*. Now, I do believe that the reading of Scripture should have a pre-eminent place in our congregational worship, though space is too short here to rehearse the theologies behind this. But preaching, although it is based on and builds on the reading of Scripture, is communication of a different kind. It is concerned with a 'forth-telling' of God's word, and has elements of the prophetic in its location in the here and now, for these people, in this place. I suggest preachers should aim to be *tellers* rather than *readers*. We tell of what we know, rather than read it from scripts. We are witnesses who have seen and heard and met with God. Furthermore, we find common ground and common parlance with contemporary people around us, rather than appearing to come from another country and another era.

Of the several New Testament Greek words translated as 'preach', *kērusso* ('herald') has a strong grip on the metaphorical imagination of many of today's preachers. However, without abrogating our responsibility to be like heralds of the truth, it has been helpfully suggested by Walter Brueggeman and others that today's believers in a post-modern, pluralist, authority-suspicious society also require *guides*.[18] They respect explorers who have been to an exciting place, a better place, and who have returned to guide and help others on the journey. These guides have the authority of experience, the advantage of recognizing the landmarks and the dangers, they have studied the work of other explorers and can usually tell good maps from bad. But their style is not that of reading, but that of sharing, of telling, of bringing forth what is inside them. This affects their embodied communication.

As well as tellers and guides, preachers should also be *imagers* – they should be able to present an image of what they mean. If you *tell* a person they must obey, improve, change, or whatever, then perhaps a small number will respond. Congratulations. You may well have created some dependents, still unable to think for themselves. *Explain* to a person how it is possible, and why it is desirable that they should obey, change and so on, then a few more might assent, though chiefly in their minds. At best, however, you only have paved the way for a later change of heart and change of practice. But show a worked example, as it were, and the listener is invited to put themselves into the picture, to find points of identification that name and release the desire at a far deeper level. Examples are conveyed by image, convincingly shared by guides, and explained and empowered by narrative.

Here's an example of what I mean. It is an extract from a sermon on Luke 17.11-19, the healing of the ten lepers. In it the preacher has imaginatively entered the scene and is telling the story, in first person monologue, of one of the nine who did not go back:

> But, back to the band of lepers, I happen to notice, as I'm on my way to show myself to the priests, that one leper who had been part of our desperate group, one of the fellow outcasts, is gone. And I look back, and I see he's with the healer, Jesus. Someone says he ran right over to him, and threw himself at his feet. And he's crying out, weeping and shouting, praising God. Well. I mean. Really. It's a disgusting display of emotion. Quite, quite unnecessary. So very un-Jewish. Not what we do in Galilee, you know. Ah, but of course. He's a Samaritan. Says it all, really. Not one of us. Worships in a different way. Doesn't believe the right things. He has a lot of the doctrine, but differs on a few points. Well, let's be honest, he differs on a few core doctrines, if you know what I mean.

> But there he is with Jesus. And Jesus is praising him for what he's doing. Jesus approves of him. It dawns on me, with burning jealousy, that this foreigner, this heretic, has something that I don't. I thought I was doing the right thing, I've always obeyed the Law, I did what the healer said I should do, and now I find I'm missing something. I'm missing something. And I don't know what it is . . .

In the narrative part of this sermon, a story is told through the first-person style. Vivid images ('threw himself at his feet') are presented. Also, by working ironically (you realize you don't want to be like the narrator) the preacher is acting as a kind of guide. Of course, the preacher has taken liberties with the scriptural narrative, which some may disapprove of. There are themes that are being raised, however, to be developed later in the sermon, themes that have arisen from a consideration of the text in its context, and what it may have meant to its original hearers. The preacher's interpretation of Luke's account of this healing is that it is one of several stories demonstrating that those who look for God's work only among those of their own nation or culture missed the point then, and the preacher is implying that the same people are in danger of missing the point now.

In Chapter 7 we will look at developing the skill of storytelling, but I want to suggest here that communicating by image and narrative is more than a rhetorical technique; it is a way of relating to culture today. This means the preparation of the person of the preacher involves being a student of communication, and how communication happens interpersonally and in community – and it also means engaging with the mass mediated communication of our culture, which leads me to my next recommendation.

Understanding contemporary culture: *Babel or Babylon?*

Karl Barth is said to have recommended preparing to preach with a Bible in one hand and the newspaper in the other.[19] An update on that would surely involve a TV on the corner, and access to Internet newsfeeds and blogs backed up by a decent broadband connection. What it emphasizes is the importance of listening to the outpourings of contemporary culture.

Culture may be defined as the sum of active, symbolic, meaning-making activities of a particular society. This means the literature and pop music, the TV and the magazines and newspapers, as well as art and architecture of all kinds. There are enormously powerful messages coming through, though they are often subtle or hidden. These messages shape people's attitudes and behaviours in ways that can be consistent with as well as opposed to the values of the gospel. Preachers need to be able to recognize and interpret what is happening in the parts of contemporary culture that are relevant to their congregations. Therefore there is no point in going lower-brow than your congregation and beware too of going higher-brow. Recognize, however, that their worlds – like yours – are shaped and influenced by the media they consume: the books, newspapers, TV, film and music.

Preaching that does not engage with the world views and unexamined assumptions swirling around our culture will be preaching that for the most part fails to connect with the concerns of most listeners. Those who listen, watch, and surf the web live in that culture for approximately seven days minus sleep time and 90 minutes or so at church each week. Congregations need preaching that celebrates the good things in culture but that also with a light touch and some skilled swordplay punctures its inflated balloons. This is a culture that so easily persuades so many of us that our body shape is wrong, that beauty and celebrity is power, that spending brings happiness, and that personal morality is about whatever feels OK. The ideologies embedded in the discourse of popular culture are powerful, and persistent, but they can be unmasked and named. To do so takes time. It takes time to engage that culture, it is not always enjoyable and it is frequently distasteful, or worse. But discernment and modelling intelligent media literacy in the pulpit can give important skills to those in the congregation who are being blown about in the winds of the media blizzard howling outside the church. In Chapter 9 we discuss some practical ways in which you can engage with the media habits of your congregation.

Honesty and self-disclosure in the sermon

Finally, how much is the person of the preacher on display in the pulpit? After reading the early parts of this chapter, you might think I am suggesting that pulpits should be filled with masses of quivering jelly (this is perhaps not an image to dwell on), vulnerably displaying their inside on the outside, and overflowing with personal testimony. By and large, this is not a good idea. If you do too much of it, as David Day remarks, 'Half the congregation want to mother you, and the other half want to send you for therapy.' Too much detail about private matters is unnecessary and distasteful, too much confession of sin or doubt undermines the authority and office of the preacher, and too much intimacy is, for the British, just too much.

Self-deprecation does go down very well in many British social situations, much more so than in the USA, for example, and a joke told against oneself is a favourite and often effective away of getting the listeners on your side. But how much to reveal of one's own doubts, fears, and sin, or indeed of success and virtuous living? There is no formula, obviously, for appropriateness of behaviour in many, many social settings. Human interaction is a matter of learning unwritten rules and codes and the ability to do this is, of course, fundamental to the range of pastoral skills required of church ministers.

Since some of us may be a little slower than others in assessing new situations, restraint is the wisest course until it becomes clear what kind of relationships we have with our listeners. If those relationships never really become clear to a preacher, as can sadly happen in some churches, then maybe it is better to preach using models of detached proclamation, didactic instruction and third-person narratives, rather than risk offence or distractions for the listener by attempting stories that are too personal. If your life does yield illustrations and examples that are too good not to use, ask yourself what is lost by recasting them as the experiences of 'a friend' or a 'person I heard of'.

A remarkable example of how appropriate self-disclosure in preaching can carry immense authority is found in a sermon by John Claypool entitled 'Life is a Gift'.[20] Claypool reflects on the story of God's call to Abraham to sacrifice Isaac in Genesis 22.1-14 in the light of the death from leukaemia, a mere four weeks earlier, of his 10-year-old daughter Laura Lue. The first thing that is immediately striking about this sermon is that whereas most honest readers of the biblical story probably get preoccupied with the question of how on earth a loving God could put Abraham through the torture of this 'test', what strikes Claypool most forcefully is Abraham's good luck – that in the end, he was allowed to *keep* his son:

> But my situation is different. Here I am, left alone on that mountain, with my child and not a ram there on the altar, and the question is: how on earth do I get down and move back to the normalcy of life? I cannot learn from Abraham, lucky man that he is. I am left to grope through the darkness by myself, and to ask: 'Where do I go from here? Is there a road out, and if so, which one?'

> Let me hasten to admit that I am really in no position to speak with any finality to such a question this morning, for I am still much in shock, much at sea, very much broken, and by no means fully healed. What I have to share is of a highly provisional character, for as of now the light is very dim.[21]

Claypool goes on, with disarming honesty, to describe two possible routes out of the darkness, which are in fact dead ends. The first is 'the road of unquestioning resignation', which he says many Christians have recommended to him. The second is 'the road of total intellectual understanding', the attempt to make absolute sense of the perplexing mix of good and evil in the world. He then outlines a third way, the only way that begins to offer any kind of hope: 'the way of gratitude'. This, he believes, is the lesson Abraham had to learn, the lesson that all we have comes to us as sheer gift from God. Here is what he says as the sermon draws to a close:

The way of gratitude does not alleviate the pain, but it somehow puts some light around the darkness and builds strength to begin to move on.

Now, having come full circle, I come back to caution you not to look to me this morning as any authority on how to conquer grief. Rather, I need you to help me on down the way, and this is how: do not counsel me not to question, and do not attempt to give me any total answer. Neither of those ways works for me. The greatest thing you can do is to remind me that life is gift – every last particle of it, and that the way to handle a gift is to be grateful . . .[22]

An example such as this does not, of course, suggest that any preacher 'ought' to feel able to preach so soon after such a tragedy. The fact that Claypool did feel able to do so, though, was itself a 'gift' of the kind he discusses. As he bears witness with complete openness to the interaction between the text and his personal grief, he gives permission to his hearers (and now his readers) to engage honestly and at the deepest level with the pain of life and death. This is the power of fitting and disciplined self-disclosure.

However, it is probably only on quite rare occasions when such levels of self-revelation are right. After all, if someone in Claypool's situation is to preach at all in the wake of such tragedy, it would be totally unnatural to speak as though nothing had happened; better, then, to be as open as possible rather than beat around the bush.

But beware of always appearing as the victim, out of control or unable to exercise authority, self-restraint, caution, or responsibility for your own life. The preacher models the Christian life for the listeners, and this requires sensitivity to what is being implicitly recommended. On the other hand, being too often the hero of the stories told becomes off-putting for many sensitive listeners, and it can be a way of dominating susceptible and immature listeners. Thus try to avoid perpetually appearing as either hero or victim of sermon after sermon. This can keep the spotlight off the preacher and on the proper subject, object and author of the sermon: God.

5

The go-between preacher

Stephen Wright

How do we decide what to say? That is the crucial question we face, whatever tradition of preaching we are at home in, whatever theology of preaching most influences our practice, and whatever shape our sermon or interactive discourse may eventually take. This decision entails an act of *interpretation*.

Different readers may respond in diverse ways to this. Some preachers take such a 'high' view of both Scripture and preaching that the idea of 'interpretation' smacks of selling out. We're not *interpreters*, they protest: we're proclaimers. Then there are preachers whose approach is so 'laid back' that 'interpretation' probably sounds too careful an activity altogether.

So my first task here is to persuade readers at both ends of the continuum and all points between that 'interpretation' is indeed what we are doing when we preach (whether we think we are or not), and that the more we are aware of it, and engaging thoughtfully in it, the more integrity our preaching ministry will have. By way of clearing the ground, here are three qualifications.

First, our 'interpretation' is not only interpretation of Scripture, but is a many-sided activity, as we shall see. Secondly, it is not something we just do 'in the study', but carries on all the way through the delivery of a sermon. Thirdly, it is not only the preacher's business. Although we approach it here mainly from the preacher's perspective, we should always bear in mind that it is an activity the whole people of God are engaged in – and not just in the reception of sermons, but in all their quest to find, do and share the will of God in the world.

To get the measure of the task, a quick reminder of some basic Christian history.

The good news of Jesus

Christianity did not start with a text, but with an event and a person. Jesus of Nazareth appeared on the scene announcing that ancient prophecies were now being fulfilled, and the time of God's rule was drawing near. This was good news for all sorts of people. And this is what triggered the Church's unending task of interpretation.

'Interpretation', at its simplest, is the effort to make sense. We put together the bits and pieces of 'data', which we receive in all sorts of ways from outside and inside ourselves, in such a way that they cohere within some overarching framework, and form a satisfying pattern of meaning. We do this not just for ourselves, in our daily processes of thought, but for others too, through our acts of communication. And what those swept off their feet by Jesus needed to interpret, when he first came and in every generation since, was his coming. What did it mean for themselves, for their understanding of God, and for the world?

The main key they had to start with was Israel's Scriptures. As the first Christians read them, they found in them the story of which Jesus was the climax. This interpretation was explored, tested and shared in oral form in the early years of the Church. In due course their own writings, in which they wrestled creatively with the meaning of Jesus in the light of the Scriptures, were collected and became 'Scripture' too. Our 'canon' of Old and New Testaments is thus itself an *act of interpretation* of Jesus' coming. It came to be recognized as the Church's main reference-point in its ongoing work of interpreting the good news.

That work was dynamic and often contested. The eventual agreement on a 'canon' of Scripture did not close down debate, or obviate the need for continuing interpretation. The 'canon' of Scripture was not intended to settle all debates about theology, philosophy, ethics or anything else that Christians and others might be discussing, but as a resource for nourishing believers in the context of worship, and instructing enquirers.[1] It was never intended to stand on its own. The Creeds, the practices of public worship and prayer, and the actual life of the Christian community all had a symbiotic relationship with Scripture, helping the Church to interpret God's revelation in Christ.

Of course, once there was a recognized 'canon' of Scripture, this became itself a part of the 'data' to be interpreted by the Church. We must now try not only to make sense of Jesus' coming, but also to understand the Scriptures that embody the early Christians' attempts to do so. This is a formidable job. The barest consideration of such a remarkable collection of books, from such a variety of literary genres, written over a period of more than a millennium, in three languages, with an undoubted but elusive oral prehistory, and a clear division between 'Old' and 'New' about three-quarters of the way through, should underline the point. Anyone who thinks that a 'correct' or 'final' interpretation of such a rich, mysterious collection can ever be arrived at is whistling in the wind. It is all the more remarkable, then, that the Church in this formative period seems not to have lost sight of the fact that its original and still primary calling as an interpreter was not merely to make sense of a text, but to make sense of a world-changing *event*.[2] In the coming of Jesus the entire cosmos, in all of its history past and future, was clothed afresh with infinite significance, which it is our human delight and vocation to explore.

Until the sixteenth century, at least, this order of priority in Christian interpretation was maintained. Scripture was a *key* to understanding what God had done and was doing in his world; it was not an object of ultimate significance *in itself*. Martin Luther expressed it like this: the Bible exists for preaching, not preaching for the Bible.[3]

The ongoing task

If this is the nature of our task, it should be clear why it is never finished and always necessary. God's entry into the world in Jesus Christ was a one-off event, but the world is constantly changing. Thus God's revelation in Jesus Christ and its communication through the Scriptures take on fresh significance when set against new developments in history. It is not that God keeps changing in a frantic effort to stay abreast of the times (as churches sometimes appear to do!) It is simply that stories and texts look and sound different to different epochs and cultures.

So, for instance, the record of Jesus' missionary charge to his little band of disciples (Matthew 10.5-42) would already have sounded different when the instructions were circulated in written form among the city churches of the Roman empire, from how they might have sounded originally to the disciples tramping the dusty lanes of rural Palestine. When Christianity became the official religion of the empire in the fourth century, and people flocked in droves to the newly built basilicas, an even greater distance would have opened up between the picture of the 'disciples' in the Gospel – a tiny group of wandering preachers – and the 'disciples' of these large settled congregations. Various 'missionary' movements down the centuries – such as those of Celts in the sixth century, friars in the thirteenth, Catholics in the sixteenth, or Protestants in the nineteenth – will have naturally felt a greater affinity with those Palestinian disciples. But still it will be seen that much has changed. For instance, any 'missionaries' today go out as part of a Church that is no longer united. Inevitably, it is not simply the 'message of Jesus' that they bring, but that message *as received and refracted within a particular Christian tradition*. And changes in cultural practice open up the distance still further. Few people today would realize the significance of a Christian minister shaking the dust off his or her feet on leaving a house (Matthew 10.14)!

The reality of a changing world does not mean that either Christ or Scripture becomes in any sense obsolete. But it does mean that the task of *interpretation* is never-ending. The Church must go on asking, what is the significance of the Christ made known in the Scriptures for our culture, our society, the world in our time? What does it mean to be a disciple *today*?

In the centuries since the Reformation, this breadth of vision has often been lost. In the divisive atmosphere of dogmatic dispute, and the defensiveness of a Church under attack from secular forces of 'enlightenment', the Bible became a weapon against opponents rather than a key to understanding God's action in the world. Whether one examined it from the perspective of Christian faith or not, for many it became merely a historical artefact to be pored over in its own right, rather than a God-given signpost helping us to make sense of what he has done and is doing.[4]

The preacher today can be in the forefront of the attempt to recapture that breadth of vision. The Bible should never have been assumed to be a monolithic knock-down answer to opponents, whether within or without the Church. Now that such monolithic knock-down answers are so decidedly out of fashion, it is a good time for us to recover the rich and subtle economy of God in which the Bible acts as means to interpret what God is doing rather than as a repository of static 'information' to be quarried for its own sake.

Interpretation is not an exact science. There will always be points at which some of our fellow-Christians sincerely disagree with us, and we with them – not to mention those of other faiths or none. So humility should pervade the whole process: a recognition of our own limitations as preachers which keeps us open to correction and thus builds again a sense of trust in the Scriptures, the Church and God himself. Moreover, it is salutary to remember that when we preach, our hearers are engaged in interpretation just as much as we are – not only of gospel, text and world, but of us! And over that process *we have no control*. Whether we like it or not, our 'interpretation' can be no more than a wager, an attempt to advance the process of understanding and transformation, bread cast upon the waters which we hope, one day, will contribute to the nourishment of human life in God's world.

Let us then set out the key elements of the preacher's 'act of interpretation' which may, in this spirit, guide preparation for each preaching event. These all contribute to what is, in a sense, a single act of interpretation. The sequence may be logical rather than temporal; the reality is that this is something we are engaged in all the time, on many levels. The process of Christian interpretation cannot be reduced to any number of 'easy steps'.

I will illustrate what follows (in this chapter and in Chapter 6) with reference to the process of interpretation I engaged in for a recent sermon on the story of Martha and Mary (Luke 10.38-42). I include this sermon (see the Appendix) not with any claim that it is representative or typical of what we should be aiming at (our discussion of the varied contexts of preaching should already have shown that this would be a foolish claim). But I do think it is helpful simply to show in a 'live' way how I am seeking to put some of what we are writing about into practice.

Dimensions of interpretation

Interpreting the good news

We reminded ourselves just now that Christianity didn't get off the ground with a text, but with a person, proclaiming and enacting good news. Our first task is to make sense of that good news for our world today.

Practically, this means that every act of preaching needs to be in some way an interpretation of the gospel. This does *not* mean that every sermon contains some formulaic 'ABC' of Christian belief, concluding with an appeal to commit one's life to Christ! The 'gospel' is more many-sided and far richer than such presentations often imply. It is, we might say, as rich as the Gospels themselves – as the New Testament itself. And its meaning is illuminated by two remarkable millennia of stories of human transformation. One could spend a lifetime 'interpreting the gospel', and have a different text or theme for each sermon. The key thing is that such preaching is not a matter of good advice or abstract theorizing, but exploring the ramifications of an *event* and the possibilities opened up by it. The question is: for any particular service, where do you start?

Each preaching event will have 'triggers',[5] one or more of which can form the starting-point for an interpretation of the good news for that day. The most common 'trigger' is simply the passage or passages of Scripture that are to be read in the service, often as part of a sequential pattern – either following an authorized lectionary, or as part of a locally planned series, or both.[6] This was the 'trigger' for my sermon on Martha and Mary: it was the Gospel reading in the *Common Worship* Lectionary for the Sunday in question. The challenge for preachers when the trigger is a biblical text is to preach it in such a way that it is *good news* for today. This is not always as straightforward as it may seem – even when it comes from the Gospels!

For example, I was aware of the well-known tradition of interpreting Martha and Mary as types of 'active' and 'contemplative' spirituality respectively – both to be honoured, but the contemplative accorded a higher place. This tradition represented a genuine attempt by an earlier Christian era to 'interpret' the text for that era. However, I was not convinced that such an understanding of the text really did justice to the 'good news' of Jesus. It suggested a two-tier model of discipleship with most people condemned to remain on the lower level. The good news as manifested here, it seemed to me, was that Mary realized, and Jesus affirmed, something which *everyone* (including Martha) could experience: that listening to Jesus and learning from him is the 'one thing' that is asked of us, and that this displaces the *anxiety* of preoccupation with 'many things'. It was not Martha's active *busyness* that Jesus challenged, but her *anxious spirit*. In the closing sentence of the sermon, in which I imagined Martha returning to the kitchen 'strangely quietened', I wanted strongly to suggest that the good news here is about the potential transformation of all our daily chores, not an unrealistic call to withdraw from them.

There are other possible triggers than the reading or readings, though it is normative for one or more texts to feature in the sermon nonetheless. An event in the Christian calendar, such as Christmas or Pentecost, carries its own logic, atmosphere and angle on the good news, which are larger than any particular text and open up rich preaching possibilities. Developments in the life of the local congregation such as building projects may trigger a sermon or series of sermons. The challenge here is that the preaching should not degenerate into mere (would-be) motivational exhortation, but remain an unfolding of the good news (the one real motivator). Thematic sermons may be preached on doctrinal or ethical matters; the danger to be avoided here is descent into abstract discussion or mere moralism. Remembering that preaching is meant to be good news should save us from this. Or a great national or international celebration, or disaster, may form the trigger. Here the key question will be: how do we make sense of the good news in the light of this?

No preacher can know just what the good news will mean for all hearers. But we can be sure of this: preaching which, over time, leaves hearers feeling demoralized, infantilized or oppressed has, indeed, lost the plot. Preaching which warms hearts and fans faith and hope into flame, whatever its inadequacies may be, is managing to hold on to it.

Interpreting Scripture

The fundamental *datum* to be interpreted is the gospel itself, but within that, the *data* of Scripture, handed down as the normative expression of Christian faith, naturally call for special attention: never as an end in themselves, but as a part of the overarching task.

Countless gallons of ink and gigabytes of disk space have been given over to the interpretation of Scripture, and therein perhaps lies the first problem for the diligent preacher, who can be overawed by the prospect of entering the fray. It is vital, then, to be confident and assertive here: a thousand commentaries may have been written on Luke's Gospel, but *no one has yet tried to make sense of this part of it for these people, on this occasion*. This might be a slightly scary and lonely thought, but it is also an exciting one. As preachers we have the high privilege of engaging in *live* interpretation. All the commentaries in the world, however 'applied' they aim to be (and many of them, often for perfectly good reasons, do not aim at this at all), have an abstract and detached feel when compared to the business of standing in front of the congregation at St Michael's or Old Street Baptist Church at 10.30 on a Sunday morning. This is *real* biblical interpretation!

It's good, therefore, to try to get one's own sense of what's going on in a text, how it relates to its context in Scripture, and its contemporary resonances, before consulting the 'experts'. But it's wise then to consult at least one or two of them. This is a matter of checking one's own insights, of entering into conversation with the Christian tradition, so that as preachers we can be effective representatives of the wider Church. In my sermon an important corrective to my thinking occurred when I consulted Joel Green's commentary on Luke.[7] I had been focusing on the social subversion of the episode, on Jesus' affirmation that 'a woman's place' is being a 'learner' with the men, not just serving in the kitchen. Green does affirm this, and it played a part in my sermon; but Green points out that the *deeper* lesson Luke seems to be teaching is not gender-related, but about hospitality itself. Mary exemplifies the truth that extending 'hospitality' to Jesus is more deeply about responding to his 'word' than it is about laying on a fine spread for him. (The 'word' of Jesus – *logos*, Luke 10.39 – is a prominent notion in Luke.) I tried to highlight this especially in my sermon.

Whatever commentaries or other books we may consult, it's good to be at home with the range of questions being asked about Scripture today in order to make sense of this unique collection. A couple of generations ago, a glance at many biblical commentaries would have shown that the questions being asked were overwhelmingly *historical*: When was this book written? What were its sources? How have they been combined? – and so on. The answers suggested were, naturally, often highly speculative, and of questionable relevance to understanding the present form of the text or its implications. Now, however, while basic historical questions about background, the meanings of words and the like remain very important, there is a widespread recognition that some of the old 'historical-critical methods' are of limited usefulness. There are all sorts of other questions to be asked if we are to make sense of these texts, and some of the best commentaries, like that of Green on Luke, engage with them.

Thus there are *social* questions about the kind of society and culture in which the characters and events portrayed in the biblical narratives take shape. An understanding of the normal role of women in Palestinian society and the wider Hellenistic world is important for interpreting Luke 10.38-42 and brings the events into relief. (We might add that this is much *more* important for us than the old historical quests such as determining the precise date of Luke, or speculating how the story was handed down to him; but that it does, of course, depend on a fundamentally historical grasp of the language and cultures of the period.) In an age when many can thankfully take it for granted that women are accepted as disciples alongside men, I felt it was important to remind the congregation of just how counter-cultural Mary's behaviour would have been.

Then there are *literary/rhetorical* questions about the structure of the biblical book and how it does its work on its readers. In this case, it is very fruitful to explore how the 'journey' motif set in train in Luke 9.51 affects our understanding of the various incidents and teachings that follow, as Jesus is depicted 'on the way' to Jerusalem. The careful reader will see how this section in effect presents discipleship as a following of Jesus on the way to the cross. The fact that Jesus is journeying also gives a special edge to the passages concerning hospitality and meals. In my sermon, I referred briefly to three other passages from this section, by way of offering a context to the story of Martha and Mary: the parallel passage in 12.14 (typical of Luke's balancing of male and female 'interest') where Jesus refuses to settle an inheritance dispute between two brothers; and 10.30-37 and 19.1-10, in which the Samaritan and Zacchaeus are presented, like Mary, as culturally 'surprising' examples of obedience.

Finally, there are *theological* questions about the text's message and its place in the unfolding revelation of God. Such questions were sometimes marginalized in the period when historical criticism ruled the day: but they are, of course, central to preaching. One area of theological investigation is the relationship between the different parts of Scripture in one 'canon'. In the sermon under discussion, I did not refer directly to other books of Scripture, but it would certainly have been possible to include some reference to the other reading for the day from Colossians 1, where Paul writes about God's commission to him 'to make the word of God fully known' (v. 25, NRSV), and especially his assertion in v. 28: 'It is he whom we proclaim, warning everyone and teaching everyone in all wisdom . . .'. A connection could be made here with Mary's listening to Jesus. Remember, though, that the lectionary readings for a particular day are not always chosen to relate closely to each other, but as part of a week-to-week sequence; so it's important not to make forced links. Also, the more texts one tries to include in a sermon, the harder the task of doing justice to them in a coherent and digestible way! Whether or not such links are made explicitly in preaching, though, the practice of having more than one Bible reading in a service helps to give a sense of the wider canvas of God's revelation, and is part of the backdrop against which the congregation will be interpreting the sermon.

I believe it's especially important that as Christians we retain a sense of our place in the great story of God's purposes stretching back to Abraham. This means that the Old Testament needs to be read regularly in worship as well as the New. It can often be helpful to link readings from both Testaments in preaching, and contemporary theological scholarship offers plenty of creative ways of thinking how to handle the Old Testament with both Christian integrity and sensitivity to our Jewish cousins.[8]

Interpreting the world

We have seen that the early Christians were convinced that the coming of Jesus had consequences for their understanding not merely of their personal destinies, but of the world as a whole. As preachers, we continue the task of helping to make sense of this world in the light of the gospel and of Scripture.

If we are to do this, we need to be *attentive* to the world around us, to the trends of culture and the strange, fascinating detail of events. It is on these that the truth of Christ needs to be brought to bear and in them that the meaning of Christ may be discerned. It is a vital part of our continuing 'formation' as preachers that we learn to be 'readers' of our world. This is not a simple business and Scripture itself warns us to eschew easy judgements. But if we do not pay attention to the world around us, we will probably end up preaching thin, stereotyped messages about a purely inward, privatized faith. God's world in all its exuberance, and pain, gives body to our speaking, and as it does so, is recognized as the object of his care.

There will be times when a current news item, popular film or cultural trend may be the actual starting-point for a sermon. More often, maybe, as in my recent sermon, the 'trigger' text will itself suggest the aspect of the world to which we need to pay attention. The obvious areas of life to which this text pointed were the relationship between work and spirituality, and gender roles. I did not devote sections of my sermon to explicit discourse on these subjects, but my awareness of them formed an essential part of the interpretative act. I knew, for instance, that I could not with any credibility advocate the contemplative life as the only serious option for Christians in twenty-first century urban Britain. More deeply, and positively, I knew that finding peace and purpose *in the midst* of sometimes frantic busyness was a cherished goal for many, sought in a variety of ways, and the suggestion that Martha was able to find this was the conclusion of the sermon.[9]

With regard to gender roles, I was aware of the potential ambiguity of the story to contemporary ears. While some reading the story with female or feminist eyes may highlight Jesus' welcome of Mary as a disciple equal to the men, others may protest at his apparent demeaning of the 'traditional' but very necessary role played by Martha. I tried to emphasize that Jesus was not demeaning this kind of necessary service; but there remains uncertainty about how my interpretation of the story might be heard as an interpretation of today's world and its conditions. Does it adequately acknowledge the oppression in which many female Martha-figures still find themselves?

We are starting to see that the issue of *how a message will be heard* is crucial to the act of interpretation. No sermon is preached into a vacuum or on to a clean slate, but takes its place in the crowded airwaves of a world full of 'messages', spoken and unspoken. No preacher can afford to ignore that world.

Interpreting the congregation

The question of how a message will be heard is, of course, most pressing with respect to the actual congregation who will be present. They, like you, are influenced in various ways by the world that you are seeking to interpret. There will also be more specific factors that will affect their reception of a message, factors which will be more or less well known to the preacher depending on his or her relationship to them.

As I prepared this sermon I was interpreting two congregations, for it would be preached twice: at an early Communion service attended by around 20 elderly people, and a mid-morning Sung Eucharist which also included the baptism of a granddaughter of a regular church member. Some writers about preaching seem to suggest that no sermon should be repeated, for each occasion is unique. While this may be true in an ideal sense, the reality is that in the midst of a busy ministry, the same 'core' message may often be preached effectively at different times and even places, but with adaptations to tone and content in response to the preacher's interpretation of the congregation both in advance and in the immediate setting.

Different parts of a message may be particularly applicable for different groups of hearers. This often needs no explicit 'flagging' in the sermon. Here, I felt that the focus on the importance of going on listening to Jesus would be helpful for the elderly congregation who probably found themselves less 'busy' than they used to be but maybe sometimes wondered how to fill their time in a purposeful way. I felt that many in the later congregation might relate more to the figure of Martha and need to hear the tone of hope and the possibility of a change of disposition in Jesus' words to her. The model Mary offered of listening to Jesus would also provide a simple yet profound example for the family of the little girl to take away with them, and practise, as they brought her up in the Christian faith, and I added a short 'epilogue' to the sermon to this effect at the later service. (It would have been harder to preach this sermon at the baptism of a boy.)

The 'vibes' both during and after the services indicated that the message was generally being received well, though of course the question of whether one has adequately interpreted one's congregation in preaching can only be adjudicated very approximately, over time. I am glad that one lady commented that she 'still had a lot of sympathy with Martha'. I am sure that the biblical authors intend to evoke our sympathy with a range of characters, including those presented as being in need of correction somehow. The point of preaching is surely not to close down discussion of a text so that the hearers 'know what's what' but to take engagement with it on to a deeper level, so that the people, situations and ideas it evokes linger with us and become more and more part of the fabric of our thinking.

Interpreting oneself

No interpretation is neutral; we come to it with all our baggage of culture, background, personality and experience. That is part of the excitement; these should be seen as positive qualities we bring to the job. But the corollary is that we should be self-aware, conscious of possible biases, blind spots and limitations. We must interpret *ourselves*. As with the other aspects of interpretation, this self-examination will be an ongoing feature of the preacher's life. We can ask: what in myself may *help* the communication of this message, and what may *hinder* it?

The first question is important because if the message does not in some way ring true to our experience, it will probably ring hollow to our hearers. Sometimes the true impact of what we are planning to say *on ourselves* may only dawn late in the day – as with the sermon I am discussing. I realized that the call to focus on the 'one thing needful', to listen to Jesus as the wellspring of all service, was a call to myself. I felt then that there was an authenticity about the message. As someone prone to anxiety, yet who has also over the years discovered the peace that comes from heeding Scripture's words on the subject, I knew that I could represent Jesus' gentle chiding of Martha to the congregation with integrity, because I realized in that moment that yet again, *I* was Martha.

The second question is important because none of us can escape from being an individual who has more 'natural' affinities with some hearers than others. But we can at least show awareness of such individual limitations and take some measures to offset them. In the case of my Mary and Martha sermon, it would have been good to think more than I did about the fact that I was a male preaching a sermon about Jesus' encounter with two females. Afterwards I felt uneasy that for some female hearers I might have left the unintended impression of a male preacher presuming to evaluate the situations of two women. This situation was compounded by my preacher's tendency to (in Fred Craddock's marvellous words) 'gravitate to the best seats in the text'.[10] The preacher identifies himself or herself almost instinctively with the character or standpoint presented by the text as authoritative or 'right', rushing to explain – even defend! – Jesus in passages like this where he can sound strange or even harsh. I tried to counter this tendency by seeing things from Martha's perspective and seeking to evoke strong sympathy for her from the outset of the sermon. Yet I ended up taking the part of Jesus and while in one sense that is natural, there is a danger of setting ourselves *over against* the congregation instead of placing ourselves explicitly *alongside* them as those whom Jesus addresses.[11]

We can never, of course, limit such unintended impressions entirely, but a careful interpretation of ourselves as a part of our ongoing preparation for preaching will enable us to grow in authentic speech and guard against unhelpful distractions from the message.

I often think of the act of interpretation as a dynamic yet subterranean business in which, like a go-between involved in negotiations between different parties, we shuttle back and forth between gospel, text, world, congregation and self.[12] Much of this goes on invisibly and inaudibly. This chapter has tried to expose it to view. We have only been able to include a single sermon by way of illustration of the issues raised, but I hope it has been enough to suggest how these issues might apply to different situations, occasions and texts. It is now time to turn to the practical task of sermon preparation. What does this subterranean activity of interpretation look like when it emerges into the busy limelight of a preacher's week?

6

Preparing to preach

Stephen Wright

What does the actual process of preparing a sermon look like? What *should* it look like? Is there advice to give, a template to apply, or is this so bound up with the personal nature of preaching – which we looked at in Chapter 4 – and the nature of the occasion, that any words we may offer here will inevitably help only some – probably a minority of – preachers?

Certainly we should keep in mind the diverse reality of 'preaching' which we have emphasized all the way through. Preparing to preach in a large church of Pentecostal tradition will be very different from preparing a message for 8 a.m. in a local rural parish church, which in turn will be very different from preparing an all-age talk for a Parade service. And the fact that preachers come from a variety of backgrounds and personality types means that there are probably nearly as many different 'methods' of preparation as there are preachers.

And yet . . . I have a hunch that certain things may need saying: things which are not so vague and general as to be useless, yet not so prescriptive as to be burdensome, or irrelevant to all but a few. I would like to consider

- the need for preparation;

- the importance of sermon structure;

- integrating the different elements of preparation.

> Geoffrey comments on how it feels to write and prepare a sermon: 'I love the testimony of the "Holiness" tradition preacher who said, "First I reads myself full, then I thinks myself straight, then I prays myself hot, then I lets myself go!" '

Why prepare?

Some might think it strange that the need for preparation requires any discussion! For them, sermon preparation is an integral, maybe time-consuming part of a week's ministry. They would certainly be alarmed at the thought of having to stand up in front of a congregation on Sunday *without* having given prior thought to what they were going to say.

Yet there are others (perhaps, unfortunately, not likely to be reading this book) who seem to make a virtue of doing a minimum of preparation (and reminding others of the fact). This is the 'a funny thought occurred to me on the way over from the vicarage' school of preaching. Though one hopes these are in the minority, the mentality they represent is based on half-truths rather than outright error. It is important to reflect on this. This mentality may even have something to teach the more diligent preparers of sermons, though they will rightly shrink from going to the other extreme. There are three half-truths in particular in need of highlighting.

The first is that *preaching is a spiritual activity, so preparation is unnecessary*. Premise true; corollary false! Just as believing in the 'fruit of the Spirit' doesn't negate the need for human effort and self-discipline – not much good fruit was ever borne from 'sit back and let it happen' Christians – so believing in the inspiration of the Spirit in preaching doesn't negate the need for preparation. A crucial part of that preparation, of course, will be precisely the *spiritual* activity of attention to God and humble prayer that he will use our words. And, indeed, the spiritual nature of the event should be remembered throughout. To emphasize preparation is not by any means to imply that the preacher should be closed off to the direct inspiration of the Spirit as he or she preaches!

The second half-truth is that *preaching is a personal activity, so preparation is unnecessary*. Premise true; corollary false! The fallacious logic here is that *personal* must imply *spontaneous*. As soon as you bring preparation into the event, so the thinking goes, you introduce an element of falsity, of artificiality, of acting. There'll be more on this idea in the next chapter. Here let's just note the element of truth in the assumption. Yes, indeed, preaching is the activity of a *person*, and if that person is unable to point as a witness to Jesus Christ through their personality and character, in the pulpit or out of it, the whole thing is aborted. A sermon that conceals the person entirely beneath a layer of cool rationality (or hypocrisy) evacuates preaching of its heart. But it is quite wrong to deduce from this that one should only utter what comes into one's head at a given moment.

Preparation of a sermon, in fact, gives far *more* opportunity for preachers to put themselves into the event than trusting to mere spontaneity, as they give their gifts and efforts of mind, heart and personality into planning an act of communication that will truly engage with their hearers. Conversely, what may well happen without careful preparation is that you fall into unconscious habits of speech, leading to the projection of a stereotyped 'you' rather than the real one. Constant refrains of 'like' and 'y' know' and 'kind of', or clicking of the tongue, may give a superficial sense that this is a 'down-to-earth guy' (of either gender), but probably become extremely irritating to most hearers if they are subjected to them on a regular basis! But, of course, preparing in advance still leaves space for elements of spontaneity when you come to deliver the sermon! This is the well-known dynamic of freedom. The child (or adult) who is given no boundaries will not know true freedom. The preacher who prepares well will have the space and confidence to feel free in delivery – to adapt, respond, express themselves freshly and genuinely when it comes to the occasion.

Thirdly, the anti-preparation lobby may assume (perhaps unconsciously) that *preaching is a pastoral activity, so preparation is unnecessary*. Once more: premise true; corollary false! Yes, preaching is a profoundly pastoral activity, and if it does not connect with and respond to and speak prophetically to the needs and situation of the congregation, a vital component is missing. And a part of this is being alert when it comes to the service, sensitive to the sudden crisis or bereavement, aware of the person who has crept in at the back whom you haven't seen in church for years, and so on. No amount of preparation can guarantee in advance that you will have the words for the moment, the words that will be right for the pastoral setting. But again, it is quite wrong to assume that this renders preparation unnecessary or even counter-productive. It is precisely in our preparation that we can both hold our listeners (whoever they will be) before God in prayer, and think how a message can be shaped that, under God, will be applicable to a range of hearers. Once this work is done, responding to the live situation is much easier.

Despite the fact that a 'don't bother to prepare' attitude tends to be based on half-truths such as these, the attitude does pose an interesting question. How big or significant does an occasion have to be before serious preparation is required for it? A part of the logic of the 'a strange thing happened to me . . .' school seems to be that you wouldn't bother to prepare in advance what to say on a routine pastoral visit, or a chance encounter in the supermarket, or if asked a question in an informal group Bible study, so why spend much effort on a sermon? It is a beguiling line of thought based on an attractive view of ministry as a seamless whole.

The answer to this logic, surely, is that different kinds of occasion call for different registers of speech, and levels of preparation, from the minister. Most ministers (and those in other public or semi-public roles) probably tend to develop an instinct for the kind of thing that is required on particular occasions. But the non-preparers do us a service if they remind us not to get too set in our ways about this. I was interested once to meet a preacher who would certainly have prepared very carefully for his sermons at the main service, in a church where Scripture and preaching were held in high regard. He told me that for the small 'early' service he did very little preparation, believing that it was a good discipline and challenge for preachers to seek to comment helpfully on a Scripture reading in a more spontaneous fashion.

So the question is, what are the occasions when careful preparation is essential? Here it's good to remind ourselves again that what we say about preaching today is meaningless without considering the theological and sociological reality of the surroundings in which it happens. Where preaching happens within a service of worship assumed to be the central, formative, focal, public gathering of the church in that place (as it most often does), it carries a particular weight. If it is obvious that little thought or care has gone into it, the formative power of the worship for the congregation will be diminished and the witness of the whole occasion spoiled. Where, on the other hand, a minister or other person is called on to speak at a more informal, smaller or less 'public' or 'normative' event, the requirement for preparation may be less, and indeed if the speaker treats the occasion in the same way as a main 'service' he or she will probably miss the mark.

The point may be made with reference to much larger or better-publicized events than most of us will ever speak at. If the Prime Minister speaks on world affairs at the United Nations or an Archbishop delivers a Christmas sermon, their words have weight and resonance far beyond the assembly building or cathedral where they are delivered. Not only their immediate hearers, but many others around the world would rightly raise an eyebrow if what they said appeared to have been merely scribbled down on the back of an envelope an hour before. The question is whether the regular gathering of God's people, in local churches week by week around the country and the world, deserves to be taken less seriously just because there are fewer hearers and the media are absent.

The discussion would not be complete, however, if we did not ask how a preacher (or any Christian) should be 'prepared' for those occasions which arise more informally and unexpectedly and which call for public words from us. Given that the boundaries between different types of church gathering may be becoming more fluid in a 'mission-shaped' Church, such occasions may be increasing. At this point we need to acknowledge that at root, the problem with preachers who do not prepare may not be simply their lack of preparation for the particular occasion. In the midst of the demands of life and ministry, after all, there will be many times when those who *do* believe in careful preparation feel they have not been able to give what they should to the task. The problem more fundamentally is when the reservoir of Christian wisdom runs dry or the channels get polluted. Jesus' promise about words being given to us in time of need (Mark 13.11) remain a great encouragement, but we should not delude ourselves that it is a charter for presumption. A preacher who really has nothing worth saying will be found out, to their own shame and, more seriously, to others' loss. And the process of being formed into people of the word, able to feed others, is far wider and deeper than a few hours thinking prayerfully and explicitly about a sermon. It is the glad work of a lifetime: a life of study, thought, prayer and learning from Jesus.

The importance of sermon structure

One of the main reasons why sermon preparation is so important is that any message needs some sort of *structure* if it is going to be truly *heard*, rather than merely enjoyed (or endured) as background noise. Let's issue the disclaimer again: God can use any sort of speech, however rambling or disorganized; but that's no excuse for ignoring the laws of good communication!

> Always preach on ONE, repeat, ONE point only, unless you have decided to be VERY textually tight. If your text requires three points, go with it, otherwise make it ONE point and develop the idea, embellish it, tell it in a story, point out other scriptures that say it differently, remind the congregation where you started and remind them of the ONE point you are making. ONE point, lovingly developed and embellished, storified, narrated, illustrated, coloured and re-told will have a chance of being remembered.
>
> Revd Douglas Holt, Bristol

Most ministers could, one hopes, without much notice stand up and give a reasonably clear and straightforward explanation of (say) the articles of the Creed and why they are important, or an interpretation of the significance of a range of well-known Bible passages, that would be more or less comprehensible at least to regular members of their congregation. But this is not the same as planning the act of communication in such a way that a particular group of hearers (or as many of them as possible – we should not get over-idealistic about this) should not only get a rough mental idea of what the doctrine or passage is about, but also be led on a journey which enables them, if they are willing, to enter into it on a deep emotional level so that it becomes *transformative* for them. For those who have been preaching for years, inevitably the same passages and themes will crop up from time to time, and this then becomes one of the main challenges of preparation: not so much to understand and interpret (though one trusts that new insights, and fresh applications, will continue to dawn, and now and again cherished views get demolished), but to communicate freshly what is 'old news' to both preacher and listeners.

The kinds of interpretation I described in the last chapter with reference to a particular sermon could, in principle, have issued in any number of different sermon structures. The one I adopted is in no sense to be taken as normative or typical or preferable to others. The very act of structuring a message is fundamentally conditioned by respect not only for the text but also for the particular group of hearers and the occasion on which one is called to preach, and that precludes there being one structure that is inherently better than another. Nevertheless, the particular sermon I preached offers a useful illustration for our purposes. It shows the influence of current thinking about preaching which encourages exploration of a variety of structures that break out of traditional discursive modes and seek to use more imaginative, narrative and dramatic forms.[1] Let me try to show here how I was striving for a structure that fitted the text, the occasion and the congregation.[2]

It is rare that the sermon form emerges from the study time – this gives the colours but the form and structure come in the space where I try to hear from God . . . Yet, of course, some passages form themselves into sermon structure from the outset – a story, repeated word/phrase or stepped argument . . .

Revd Oliver Ross, London

First, it is good to have a structure for the sermon that is appropriate to the text being preached on. This in itself is a significant discovery (or more likely rediscovery) in thinking about preaching in recent years. There is something constricting and in the end manipulative about squeezing every text into a sermon of three (or four, five or six) points – as has sometimes happened in certain circles! Coming to a text *expecting* to preach on it in this way can block our own hearing of the text in its own terms, and therefore the congregation's hearing of it. Thus there is something natural about using narrative forms to preach on a narrative text, and that is what I did here with the Mary and Martha story. I tried to help people place themselves in the story, taking Martha's perspective, and imagine their way through from beginning to end.[3]

It would have been quite possible to take a different tack altogether and still remain sensitive to the narrative form of the text. For instance I could have centred the sermon on the words of Jesus 'one thing is necessary' and used these as a refrain. This would still have allowed some imaginative development of the characters of Martha and Mary as well as the inclusion of present-day examples of anxiety and trust. Respecting the form of the text does not imply that one should follow its contours slavishly. Rather, it's a matter of catching the spirit of it. A sermon on a narrative text that allows the hearers to sense nothing of the movement of the plot, nor feel any empathy or sympathy or antipathy towards any of the characters, nor see any of the colouring of the setting and background, surely does Scripture (and the hearers!) poor service.

It is important to counter any notion that experimenting with different sermon structures is some fancy indulgence that entails 'departing from Scripture'. It is one of the key aims of searching for the right structure that we should stay *closer* to the text, not veer away from it. No sermon can or should reflect the text exactly; central to the preaching enterprise is that the text's message should be related to a particular group of hearers, and that means that the text on its own is not sufficient to suggest the right structure. It is the unthinking adoption of 'standard' sermon patterns that is more likely to sit loose to the text than the careful search for an appropriate structure. The different types of biblical literature – narrative, law, wisdom, poetry, epistle and so on – may each suggest a range of possible sermon forms which respect the genre and catch the mood.[4]

I think having tried to grasp the meaning of the passage as a whole, but before trying to break it down into a logical sequence, or a series of points, I will ask myself: what is the issue here? i.e. what is the overall thrust of the application I sense this sermon will convey?

Revd Duncan MacLaren, Edinburgh

Second, it is important to seek a structure for the sermon that fits *the occasion*. I give this separate treatment from 'the congregation', because I am not simply thinking of the people who will be at the service, but the nature of the service itself. As suggested in Chapter 2, every service is imbued with certain expectations, traditions (often unacknowledged as such), and (often) unspoken assumptions about 'why we are here' and 'what we do'. There is a complex and subtle dynamic at play in which the main carriers of that church's tradition – the ministers, leaders or inner core of members – shape an act of worship in which, maybe, a wide range of others participate, including those whose assumptions, expectations and knowledge of the 'tradition' may vary widely from those of the main 'carriers'. In human terms, one of the main factors enabling the preacher's act of communication to 'work' will be the extent to which he or she has the measure of this dynamic.

My sermon was preached in a church with a 'liturgical preaching' tradition in which the ministry of the word is seen as being closely bound up with the ministry of the sacrament. As we saw, the focus of such preaching is in facilitating the encounter of the worshipper with God through renewing their sense of some aspect of his good news. This is not mere preaching 'to the in-crowd', for the worshippers are not seen as a race apart. There is a healthy blurring of the congregation's boundaries. People drift in (and, yes, out). The hearers, in other words, are seen as representative of humanity as a whole. That means that the preacher tries to speak a language that is accessible to all, even if sometimes the mysteries of God call for expressions that are strange and evocative rather than merely 'easy'.

In such a setting I aim for a message that will be relatively brief, aiming to touch mind, heart and will with an aspect of the gospel that is central to one (or occasionally more) of the biblical texts that have been read. In another setting, where the tradition is of a longer 'teaching' sermon, I would have gone into more detail about the background of the story, its position in the Gospel, the connection with other passages and so on (though all still with an eye to its transformative impact, and therefore succinctly and selectively: no sermon, I believe, should be a mere dispensing of information). The key thing is that the 'fit' of the structure with the occasion is more important than my personal preferences or tastes.

The *position* of the sermon in the service will suggest some basic elements of its structure. In the Anglican tradition, the sermon at Holy Communion comes immediately after the Gospel reading. This means that the preacher has an immediate launch-pad. The reading will pose questions, arouse feelings, bring back memories, sometimes cause uneasiness. It is precisely that sense of what is likely to be going on in the congregation's hearing of the text that often gives the preacher the most natural clue to an appropriate structure for the sermon. In my sermon, I aimed to tap immediately into the sympathy for Martha, which I imagined – I think correctly! – would be the instinctive response of most hearers to the story. Having decided on this opening, the rest of the structure more or less suggested itself. This is not to imply that there could not have been other starting-points; nor that the Gospel reading should always be the focus. It's simply to point out how when you think about the sermon as part of the occasion, a possible structure may start to emerge quite naturally. If it had been a different sort of occasion, quite a different structure would have been called for. For example, at a 'guest' service with an address towards the end focusing on a Christian response to an issue of the moment, like global warming, it would be natural to start with a story or image related to the topic, and devise a structure which allowed one to build up to a succinct exposition of a key biblical text. Special occasions such as civic services, marriages and funerals – important events which we do not have space to discuss in detail – have a logic of their own which may suggest appropriate sermon structures.

A word needs to be said about the sacramental context of this particular sermon, on both occasions when it was preached – and of many sermons that readers of this book will be preaching. Some advocates of 'liturgical preaching' imply that every sermon must somehow lead up to or refer to the celebration of Holy Communion, which is the focus of the gathering. Such a focus would, of course, impose something of a ready-made structure, or at least an end-point. My own feeling is that one can (and should) always be mindful of the sacramental context in preparing a sermon structure, but that it is not necessary always to be explicit about it. As with the other elements of the service – songs/hymns, prayers, parts of the readings not addressed explicitly – the connection between sermon and sacrament can be allowed to emerge in echoes, rather than be laboured.

In this case, the theme of hospitality and meals in the Gospel reading (and throughout Luke) could well have provided a link to the Eucharist, and on another occasion I might have made it explicitly. Even staying within the narrative structure, a reference to welcoming Jesus and hearing his word at the 'feast' where we honour him could have been woven in. The main reason I did not do so this time was because the second service was also a service of Holy Baptism. I knew that a number of visitors, perhaps not regular church-goers, would be present, and I did not want to make the symbolic freight of the narrative too complex. Nor did I think it necessary to go into the meaning and theology of baptism: the words of the service themselves proclaim this, and detailed exploration of it by those most closely involved is likely to be much more fruitful in a relaxed setting in the parents' home with a minister or baptism visitor, than in the service itself with restless children and adult nerves on edge! In a few words after the sermon I led into the baptismal liturgy by pointing to Mary's example of listening to Jesus as one for the baby girl to be taught to emulate as she grew up. (It would have been better for this to have been woven into the structure of the sermon itself; people could tell that the 'sermon proper' had ended and started shifting in their seats and getting out their orders of service!)

The third key element that will suggest how a sermon can be structured is the congregation themselves. A preacher who is at least reasonably familiar with the likely hearers – or if not with all of them personally, at least with their dominant culture(s) and backgrounds – will be able to develop a sense of what is likely to 'work' as an act of communication, and what won't. Naturally there is always a healthy element of experimentation here. I had tried a directly narrative approach once or twice with this congregation before, and it seemed to 'connect', as I think it did this time. Sometimes congregations have very fixed notions of what shape and style a sermon should have – notions that have no doubt been imparted and reinforced by the sermons they have actually heard over the years! In such cases, it is important not to ride roughshod over people's expectations, but equally important not to be hidebound by them. For example, some members of a congregation that has been used to detailed verse-by-verse exposition might have been aghast if the sermon I've been discussing had been preached to them. You can imagine the comments: 'not much more than a "thought for the day"! We want more meat than that!' I would want to respect the tradition and expectations of such a congregation (as of any Christian congregation), recognizing that any structure that helps people to hear God speak is helpful, and may be enriched. A verse-by-verse exposition can be enlivened by the use of imagery and story – just as a narrative approach can incorporate succinct elements of explanatory background. At the same time, sermon structures can become a subtle form of idols. If people think, perhaps unconsciously, that they can only hear the word of God when it is presented as – say – a story, *or* when it is presented as three points and a poem, or whatever, they need to be disabused of the idea. This can be an important subject for continuing pastoral education, and there are welcome signs around that Christians across the spectrum of traditions are opening up to less familiar patterns of preaching.

Integrating the elements of preparation

All that has been said about preaching so far underlines the fact that preparing a sermon is very far from being a mere matter of assembling information in a coherent order, ready to be read out at the appropriate time. Preaching is an oral event, and potentially a rich moment of divine–human and human–human encounter that may take everyone, including the preacher, by surprise. 'Preparing' a sermon is not a matter of having it safely 'sewn up', but of preparing oneself, before God, for that moment.

The number one priority by a long way, for me, is to get the text for the sermon up on the screen (after reading it in its context in a real Bible), in Greek and a couple of translations, or if OT then two to three English versions. Then I print it out and carry it around all week. I ask the Lord to speak through it for the sake of those who need to hear his Word (and that includes the preacher).

Revd Fleming Rutledge, New York

This means that 'preparation' cannot be confined to a set number of hours (more or fewer depending on your background and personality!) spent in a study. The reality is at once more demanding and more liberating than that. Preparation can be happening all the way through the twists and turns of a busy pastoral week – or a busy week in 'secular' employment. As suggested in Chapter 4, the crucial insight that will bring the sermon to life may dawn not in the study but on a walk by the canal – or, it may be, sitting at a hospital bedside or taking a phone call in the office.

Let's look at five key elements of preparation, armed with this reminder that in healthy preaching practice they will be closely interwoven.

> I seek a space where I can hear from God. As the week progresses if I don't hear I become more desperate. If nowhere else I go and stand under the shower – the best place is the sea shore for me but that's not always possible . . .!
>
> Revd Oliver Ross, London

The first element must surely be *prayer*. This should not be heard as a trite point, nor as a demand for hours on one's knees. We saw in Chapter 3 that God is a central player in the event of preaching – which does not imply that we have a hot line to him, or that we can somehow manipulate his presence, but rather that he promises to continue to speak to his children, and that we can humbly ask him to do so, however he pleases. So prayer in preparation for preaching is to acknowledge that it is God's word alone which brings life, healing and hope to humanity, and to ask simply that our words will be vehicles of his word. Such prayer will naturally come to explicit focus at certain key moments in the whole process: especially as we start consciously to think about it, immediately before the sermon is preached, and in the aftermath. But between those times it will continue to find expression, wordlessly, in the attitude of wonder and openness that recognizes our limitations and gives space for the mysterious nudges and invisible workings of the Spirit.

> I go through the passage four separate times, four different ways. I usually do 15 minutes for each segment. First, I go through the passage with the mind, noting the who, what, where, when, etc., just fixing the facts of the passage in my mind. Secondly, I go through the passage with the body, using my five senses. Thirdly, I go through the passage with my feelings, especially entering a character's point of view. Finally, I go through the passage with my spirit, asking the question – what is God saying to me through this text?
>
> Ron Boyd-Macmillan, Edinburgh[5]

The second element is *study*. God has given us minds with which to contemplate him, his word and his world, even though we shall never fully grasp them. In Chapter 5 we discussed the act of interpretation, the business of making sense of God's good news in the light of Scripture and for the benefit of today's world. If we are to take this seriously, this *will* entail time spent in reading, specifically focused upon the task of preaching. The reading will be of Scripture and of whatever other material can shed light on it for us, and can help us to see how its ancient message has continuing power today. But it will also be of the 'texts' of today's culture – films, novels, poetry, painting, blogs – whatever gives us a window on to the human world for whom we are called to interpret. As with our prayer, the attitude will be one of humility. We will never in this life attain the ultimate, 'correct' interpretation of any text or any cultural artefact. Our calling is to bear witness to that which we see and hear, remaining constantly open to new shafts of light upon the truth.

It is vital that I am continually noting films, books and encounters during the week that affect, though they may not directly shape what I say.

Revd Jock Stein, Kincardine

This leads to our third element: *observation*, of the corners of the world in which we move, and especially of the people among whom we live and work. Such observation will not be crude voyeurism, or merely shallow picking-up of 'illustrations'. It will, rather, be a matter of profound attention to the world *in which* God speaks and *to which* he still wants to speak. This 'observation' is not merely visual, but involves all the senses. If we are observant like this, our reading will be immeasurably enriched through immediate experience and insight. Most importantly, we will deepen our sense of the real needs and longings, virtues and vices, glories and neuroses of the human family of which we are a part, so that we grow gradually in our equipment to address them with the right words of affirmation or confrontation.

The fourth element will be *thinking*: exploring the lines of illumination that travel both ways between Scripture and culture, the mutual links between our reading and our observation, and putting our creative powers to work to see how just a few of these manifold connections can be made to buzz with life in the encounter between preacher and congregation.

The final element is *self-discipline*, which is both a moral and a psychological matter. We have seen that the person of the preacher cannot be bypassed. This does not mean that the preacher is called to aspire to (still less, claim!) a level of 'perfection' that is quite unrealistic. It does mean that there is a particular requirement on those called to give *public* articulation of the good news to be transparent in their personal faith and engagement with that good news. Words are vital, but they are only the tip of the iceberg. As Jesus knew, what we say issues from deep wells within. If we take seriously this need for integrity, that will prevent us from mouthing glib platitudes or easy assurances.

In the sermon I have been discussing, I hope that I did not give the impression that overcoming anxious distraction and learning to listen to Jesus was easy, because I know personally that it is hard. The occasion did not allow detailed expansion of the theme, but another time, as appropriate, I would be prepared to go to some lengths to explore the roots of anxiety in our stress-filled contemporary way of life, and some of the remedies proposed by modern psychology which may sound quite 'unspiritual' yet are surely a part of a God-given order of things which we have often forgotten. I would not be happy to preach on Jesus' words about anxiety and worldly cares if I thought they were hopelessly unrealistic (I have heard one or two highly unsatisfying sermons which seemed to imply as much); but nor would I ever wish to preach on them without taking seriously the new insights into anxiety and ways of dealing with it which contemporary medical science has brought to light.

Self-discipline in preparation, then, is first a matter of maintaining an integrity of life which brings together faithful testimony to the gospel as it has been handed down to us, and honesty to our own experience and the insights into the fabric of life which come to us from many quarters. But it also concerns the more practical matter of psychological preparation for the dynamics of the preaching event itself. There is, as we shall see in the next chapter, an inevitable element of performance about this event, which calls for a fitting degree of psychological preparedness. Partly this is a matter of taking time to internalize the core message, so that one is free to speak it out rather than read it, and to adapt it as may seem right at the time. There are different schools of thought about the use of a script. The production of a script beforehand seems to me essential for all but those with extraordinary powers of memory,[6] though the way in which it should be used in the event itself (if at all) will vary depending on the preference of the preacher.

> Computer composing is my way in to a sharper realization of what I had previously apprehended only vaguely.
>
> Revd Dr David Schlafer, Washington DC

But beyond internalization of the message, there is the deeper kind of psychological preparation for the event itself. Again, the nature of such preparation will vary considerably depending on the personality of the preacher. For example, the natural extravert may take the whole event much more in their stride than the natural introvert, for whom the instinctive thought of appearing before a congregation may be initially threatening. For all preachers, a sense of the significance of the occasion and the privilege of being caught up in it will surely produce a healthy sense of anticipation. As the psychologists remind us, eliminating anxiety altogether would not be good: a certain minimum level is necessary if we are to give of our best! But as suggested in Chapter 4, this should surely not take on undue proportions, squeezing out the possibility of spontaneity and joy. It is not healthy to be so hypersensitive before preaching that the slightest uncertainty about the message, wayward thought, cloud in a relationship, or irritation with something or someone in the service throws you off balance.

All these elements, then – prayer, study, observation, thought, self-discipline – combine in not always predictable ways in sermon preparation. It is clearly not a chronological sequence. There are some elements of logical order in it – for instance, many (though not all) would argue that it is good to have a clear idea of what you are going to say before the stage of thinking how to say it.[7] But it is a dynamic process that, overall, it is unhelpful to try to over-regulate. Moreover, it is primarily a matter of regular habit rather than of narrow focus on a specific sermon, though sooner or later time does need to be carved out for that narrower focus. And running through all the elements is the golden thread of humble anticipation: readiness to learn, to see, to discover: above all readiness to be encountered by God and to *be* a particular kind of person – a go-between, in ways known to us and unknown, in his encounter with others.

Geoffrey adds, 'I also like the advice given to me by a former colleague in Durham, Bob Fyall, now Warden at Rutherford House, Edinburgh, and renowned for his gripping and brilliant expository sermons. The best advice for sermon writing he had was, "Find your own brand of murder, and get away with it!" '.

7

The act of delivery

Geoffrey Stevenson

Truth, or artifice?

I bring to my practice and study of preaching nearly 20 years' experience in the theatre as an actor and director, and I love to observe the connection between acting and preaching. Despite the sense you often get that some preachers are giving a theatrical performance in the pulpit, many would want to draw fundamental distinctions. Isn't it the job of the preacher to handle truth, while the actor deals in pretence and dissembling? Doesn't the preacher stand alone and vulnerable in the pulpit, while the actor is aided by artifice, dependent on the inventiveness of the playwright, the decorative skills of the designer, not to mention the devious craft of the make-up artist? The actor is known for playing a part, for being someone else, for speaking lines others have written, for wearing a mask, for being the ultimate hypocrite. The preacher crafts his or her own words, and perhaps has more in common with the political orator, attempting to persuade and convince, drawing from strength of conviction and most of all a desire for the truth that is inspired by God.

Well, you might think so. But a deeper look at both the craft of acting and the art of preaching may show us that there are some important connections, and that the preacher can learn much from the actor.

Perhaps common ground resides in a powerful voice, or exaggerated facial expressions, or making gestures large enough to be seen? Yes, but there is more, much more to it than that. While the finely judged control of voice and body is integral to the craft, behind them lies the motivation for any action or line of dialogue. The best actor searches for truth with a driving hunger and consuming dedication. The line on the page or the gesture in the air is only a start, and it is merely a vehicle for transporting truths from the writer to the audience. These are truths of what it is to live, love, laugh, believe, suffer, sin and experience grace. An audience is not likely to apprehend such truths unless and until the actor has first found a way of connecting with those truths both emotionally and physically, in voice, movement and gesture.

In Stanislavski's *An Actor Prepares* [1] the pioneering Russian director tells the story of an actress in his school who played a scene in which she frantically, extravagantly and unsuccessfully searched for a valuable brooch pinned to a curtain. The results were superficial and melodramatic, although she finished the exercise flushed with emotion and convinced she had done well. The director informed her that there was still a brooch there, and that unless she found it, she would have to leave the school and could no longer attend the classes. This time her search was convincing, her disappointment intense.

'Oh, where is it? Oh, I've lost it.' The words were muttered in a low voice.

'It isn't there,' she cried, with despair and consternation, when she had gone through every fold. She had forgotten about acting, and the rest of the class were riveted by her performance. The director then makes her see how truthful her performance was the second time, for she had touched emotions and motivations that really existed.

The actor sometimes must dig deep into himself or herself to find the true motivation, drawing not on what he or she has personally experienced – that would be far too limiting – but on what his or her *empathetic imagination* can tell him or her about what it looks and feels like, for example, to sit down in a chair struggling to process the news that a tragic accident has just occurred, or to greet with required politeness someone who means to bring nothing but harm. Falsehood and superficiality will not do here. The actor is not a blank slate, which the director and playwright use for their scrawls, but an active agent whose effectiveness depends on the ability to get at the truth.

The subtitle of this chapter could be 'A preacher prepares'. That preparation has as much to do with learning to be real and truthful about his or her relationship to the message that is going to be preached as it has about techniques to ensure that he or she can be seen and heard. Preachers often think they deal, not in little truths, but in Truth, that is, God's self-revealing action of grace in which the preacher is no more than a mouthpiece. That is not the understanding of preaching in this book. At every level of the preaching event, the preacher should be asking, true or false?

What kind of falsehood tempts me when I have practically to drag myself into the pulpit, pretending to feel enthusiasm for words and 'truths' that have lost their meaning and importance for me? Is it truthful to point the finger (metaphorically, of course) with superficial moralizing or guilt-inducing exhortation that I do not apply to myself? How true is an elaborately constructed conceptual and rhetorical tour-de-force that has nothing to do with the social, ethical or psychological realities of the day-to-day lives of my listeners? It is a hard question, but I have to ask it: 'Am *I* being true, or false?'

Telling tales

In this book we have emphasized the importance of story to preaching. In our chapter on the person of the preacher in particular (Chapter 4) it was suggested that the lifelong development of a preacher should involve the understanding of story, and a self-perception as a storyteller who acts as a guide and who is able to paint pictures with words. What this means for the delivery of the sermon is terrifically important.

Outside of the church, one of the dominant models of information giving is the TV presenter. Authoritative, and yet approachable. Slick (working from autocue) and yet friendly. An everyday man or woman, yet in command of slides and video clips called up in an instant. Now we may not have (or want to have) the resources of the TV presenter, and may resist to the death the packaged and rehearsed slickness, with all its artificiality. So in order not to succumb to the trap of overly smooth delivery, we should aim at authentic, approachable, conversational styles of speaking.

The best way I have found to learn to work in the modes of teller, guide and imager is to practise as a storyteller. If you have ever had the pleasure of reading stories to small children, you have made a start. Even more relevant are times in social situations, around a table or in a small group, swapping tales and incidents.

Activity

Listen attentively to the stories, incidents and anecdotes that you hear in everyday situations as they are told by friends, relatives and colleagues. Note the qualities and techniques (even if used unconsciously) that distinguish good storytellers from poor ones. Choose one such quality or technique and aim to incorporate it into a story the next time it is your 'turn'. This may feel false or strange, but with practice it can become natural and habitual.

Storytellers learn to keep the attention of the listeners by painting verbal pictures, by using words economically and appropriately, by letting their voice reflect the energy and emotion of the story, and by seeming to draw the incident or tale from their own experience or imagination. The story is not recited by rote, nor read dryly from a book, but it is *told*. Storytelling is a developed folk-art form, with a good body of literature and many organizations and practitioners devoted to it. At this point I can only urge you to look at some of the books in the Resources section,[2] and to take it further in your life. Read about storytelling, research storytelling, but above all, tell stories as you tell The Story, in and out of the pulpit.

And how will they hear?

In contemporary public speaking, it is nearly always advisable to try to produce 'a voice that is heard, but that never declaims'. The preacher has no use for a voice that calls attention to itself. You will have heard it: an 'ac . . . tor's' voice, with *basso profundo*, sibilant sss's, crisp consonants, and drawn out vowel sounds. How artificial. How very un-British. As Jana Childers observes, 'to most listeners it is more important that a speaker be natural than almost anything else'.[3] Yet this should not deter the preacher who seeks a more professional approach to the craft of public speaking. Be honest: don't we dislike such vocal display because we suspect that a 'showman' resides in the speaker? Barring acquired habits of which the speaker is patently unaware, the humility and godliness that would directly counter such a flaw have nothing really to do with the voice, and everything to do with character and integrity, and that is the concern of a different chapter in this book. For now I propose that it is the responsibility of the preacher (as of any professional speaker, but most especially when doing it 'for God') to honour God and the listener by paying full attention to excellence in technique that assists in effective ministry.

However, a person's voice is tremendously personal. It expresses who they are in particular ways, and in the tremors, variations and responsiveness to context it is intimately revealing. Many people are extremely sensitive to criticism and resistant to working with their voice. Some people have said to me that they would rather have their face criticized than their voice. Consciously or intuitively, they are wary of sounding artificial or unnatural. For this reason, some voice trainers and speech therapists speak of 'freeing the voice' rather than training it, underlining its intimate connection with personality. But whatever the terminology, personality can and should be respected. Childers again: 'Being natural and being effective are not mutually exclusive goals.'[4]

There is much to be learned from listening to great preachers and speakers of the past, such as Martin Luther King and Winston Churchill, but quite clearly it would be of no use at all to imitate their style of speaking (even if you *could* approximate the resonant musicality of King's voice or the gruff and resolute conviction conveyed by Churchill). Most audiences in twenty-first-century Europe – and I include congregations just this once in this category – are used to an altogether more down-beat and low-key style of speaking, closer to the naturalism practised by stand-up comedians. Even when playing the biggest theatres in the country, the use of a wireless microphone strapped to the side of their heads allows many of these comedians to speak very conversationally, as if you were sitting having a drink with them.

Having said that, the crucial question to ask is, 'what is my speech trying to achieve?' If it is speech intended to bolster a nation's spirits in time of war, or rally a huge crowd to mobilize in support of racial equality, then chatty stories, asides and throw-away lines are not appropriate. Clearly, preaching is aiming for something that is of a different order from either the heroic leader or the funny man at the pub, but does that mean sounding like he comes from a different planet? It's all about register. The preacher needs to identify the right register(s) for speaking, and then develop the techniques for working within that. This task can only really be done through attention to real-world situations, but some initial pointers may be helpfully laid out here.

A preacher's voice should be developed or freed in five areas, the first three of which are more specifically associated with the sound producing mechanisms of mouth, throat and lungs, and will be the focus of the exercises in the rest of this chapter:

1. *Voice quality* This is a function of volume and resonance along with articulation and enunciation. These combine to cause the voice to be heard over other noise and distractions. They form the ability to 'project' the voice over distance and in large buildings. It is related to but distinct from:

2. *Musicality* or its tonal range, and the use of pitch, pace and timing. These contribute to its ability to communicate inflections in the spoken word, to hold the listener's attention and to make sounds that are pleasing rather than wearing to the listener.

3. *Control* and stamina, which are principally functions of breathing.

The other two areas of vocal development are more properly associated with achieving the appropriate register of speech, as discussed above.

4. *Expressiveness*, in other words the voice's ability or capability to express faithfully the intention, attitude and emotion of the preacher.

5. *Manner of speaking* or rhetorical use of language. Not strictly about voice, but about speech and the way it is heard. Inextricably linked to the context and congregation, it includes repetition, contrasts, use of metaphor and example, and other ways to give emphasis to and make memorable what is being said.

I have said that voice quality is a part of projecting the voice, for it requires more than increasing the volume. Indeed, shouting actually decreases the effectiveness of the voice in several important ways. It also leads very rapidly to strain and damage to the vocal chords. If you merely push your voice to go for more sound, these things are likely to happen:

- Your voice will go up in pitch, compressing your available range for expression and also becoming more tiring for the listener.

- The sound will come out all at the same pressure, again assaulting the ears of the congregation. Remember that excessive volume can be as wearing as a voice that is too faint.

- The resulting tension in the neck restricts the throat, cutting out lower tones and 'chest notes', thus further negating inflections in the words.

- The listener becomes more aware of the sound than of the word.

Public speaking should nearly always be effortless, a product of trained muscles, good ingrained habits and effective breath control. Therefore it is important to have a programme of exercises, repeated over time, in order to develop good habits and to strengthen and maintain the muscles involved in voice production.

Breath control

The lungs may be taught to produce and push the air that flows across the vocal chords with great control, and to draw in breath that is needed with speed and efficiency.

Most people most of the time breathe from the upper chest, signalled by the collarbone rising and falling.

> Try that now, by placing your fingertips on the front of your collarbone, to one side or the other of your neck. Observe what kind of movement occurs as you breathe, both naturally, and when you try to take in and expel especially large breaths.

Typically not much more than a third of the air in the lungs is changed with each breath. This limits the amount of air that can be expelled past the vocal chords to produce sound. A long line of text cannot be sung or spoken without stopping for breath, often interrupting the phrasing inappropriately. The amount of oxygen available for strenuous activity is limited. There is not much strength available to push breath out with the force needed to project the voice.

Active breath control begins with identifying and breathing abdominally. This means utilizing the diaphragm, a wall of muscle separating the lung cavity from the abdominal cavity.

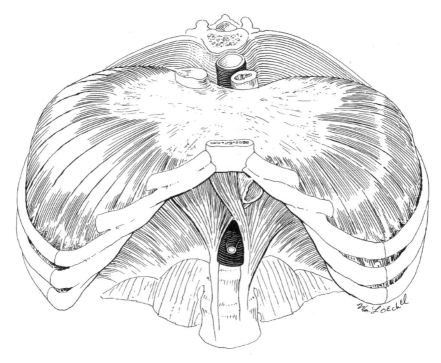

Image: Walters Kluwer Health Inc., reproduced with permission

Largely used involuntarily, the diaphragm can be felt in action during hiccups, propelling the air from the lungs in a series of spasms. But the actor and singer, preacher and public speaker learn to use it propel air out and draw breath in with much greater power and much finer control than breathing from the upper chest. Greater volumes of air are exchanged, with a control that can make all the difference, when singing or speaking, to being able to arrive at an appropriate point in the text before having to draw breath.

The following exercise may assist in identifying and learning to utilize the diaphragm consciously.

Imagine you are trying to make a fog on a cold window pane – open your mouth wide, lean slightly forward and breathe out strongly. If there is not a cold window to hand, try it with a large empty glass. Another method is to go down on your hands and knees and pant, rapidly with short breaths. It is difficult to do these while breathing from the upper chest.

Correct and controlled breathing is also an important component in managing the stress that can be brought on by the fear or anxiety of public speaking. If this afflicts you at all, then in addition to prayer, try to:

- Stand or sit upright, with head upright, face forward and the shoulders straight.

- Release tension in neck and shoulders with gentle movements: lift and lower the shoulders; rotate the shoulders forwards and backwards, individually and together.

- Take deep breaths (not so deep that you hyper-ventilate), breathing in through the nose, and exhaling through the mouth.

Exercises for developing and maintaining projection, articulation and breath control

The following exercises are the merest sampling of the kind of programme that is needed to develop the voice. If a convenient series of voice classes cannot be found, then there are a number of excellent and practical books, which I recommend in the Resources section. In all cases, repetition of exercises is crucial. They should be done methodically and repeated regularly until basic skills are developed and good habits initiated. Thereafter, they should form part of a warming-up process prior to speaking in public.

- Breath control exercise: Count out loud slowly from 1 to 12, maintaining the same volume and pitch for each number. (Try to do this on one lungful of breath, so that you finish as strongly as you began without either running out of breath or having a lot of breath left over.)

  When this can be done comfortably, count up to 16 at the same pace, pitch and volume. Then 20. Then 24.

  Repeat this exercise every few days and you will increase your breath control dramatically, although real success will not come until the diaphragm is engaged in the process.

- Yawn several times, with the mouth *closed*.

- Make a vigorous chewing motion with the mouth *closed*, to exercise the jaw muscles.

- Limber up the lips and tongue by rapidly pronouncing the following consonants:

  PPPPP PPPPP
  TTTTT TTTTT
  KKKKK KKKKK
  LLLLL (say 'la', moving the tongue from top to bottom of the mouth for each)
  Ch Ch Ch Ch Ch Ch Ch Ch
  FFFFF FFFFF (say 'fa')
  SSSSSS SSSSSS (say 'suh')

- Yawn again, normally, and while yawning, gently sing a variety of notes. (Note how the sound quality changes with the beginning and end of a yawn and the subsequent changes of mouth shape and jaw position.)

- Speak the following line, emphasizing the vowel sounds, and exaggerating the shape of the lips:

  WHO WOULD KNOW AUGHT OF ART MUST LEARN, THEN TAKE HIS EASE[5]

  Note how the position of the lips changes, as they draw back more and more with each word.

- Volume exercise 1: Count to 10 with increasing volume, from a very faint '1' to the loudest possible '10', and back down again. Be sure not to change pitch while changing volume

- Volume exercise 2: Repeat a short phrase, such as 'Building a church takes time and patient prayer' getting progressively louder with each repetition, in the following stages: whispered / softly / conversationally / projected / loudly calling. Then reverse the progression, going from a shout to a whisper.

Voice care

Voice care is a way of protecting that part of the body without which the job cannot be done. Actors, singers, and those whose livelihood depends on regular usage of their voice, develop techniques and habits to protect their voice. Here is a brief introduction to some of them:

1. Learn to work habitually within your tonal range (which you discover and gradually extend through voice development).

2. Produce the sound from the correct part of the body (which means breathing from the diaphragm and understanding resonance – again, develop the voice in a programme of practical exercises).

3. Produce sound while standing with correct posture. Be aware especially of the position of the neck, making sure that it is not strained or pushed into an unnatural position, for this will produce tension in the throat.

4. Keep the vocal chords lubricated. Drink plenty of (non-caffeine/non-alcohol) liquids when using the voice. Regular steam inhalation, morning and night, can be especially beneficial at a time of great demands on the voice. Have water to hand when talking so you can take regular small sips to keep the throat moist.

5. Rest your voice when it is tired or if you have strained it.

6. In cold weather and when there are colds and flu germs about, wrap up the throat when going out and wear a muffler, to reduce the amount of very cold air flowing through the nose. The cold air stimulates blood flow into nasal passages, which restricts the airflow but also makes them more vulnerable to viral infection.

7. Warm up the voice before use, rather than bellowing out the first hymn in a cold church early in the day. The following exercise I consider invaluable.

The Siren
A simple voice warm-up exercise.
(If you are not alone when you try this out, chances are you will be not long after you start!)

It may help to imagine a small boy (or girl) playing with a toy fire engine. It is well early, before parents are supposed to be wakened, and the siren is the sound he makes, very, very quietly, as he runs his toy along the floor. The sound comes from the top of the mouth, with the back of the tongue pressed against that area (known as the soft palate), as if the *ng* (as in *sing* or *rang*) sound were being made, without a vowel sound. Vary this sound in pitch, smoothly and ever so quietly going to the top of your range and back down to the lowest note you can reach. Repeat several times. You may get some strange looks in the vestry, but your voice will have a better chance of fulfilling the demands soon to made upon it, and be better protected against strain leading to hoarseness, loss of voice or worse.[6]

The voice should not be thought of as an external instrument, manipulated for the purpose of speaking: the connection between thought : intention : speech is too complex and intimate. Similarly, fitting your voice to a situation is not done mechanically, but holistically. This final exercise may help and illustrate:

Breathe the space

When addressing a group of people, just before your opening words, and after you have stood up or arrived at the position from which you will speak, take one good breath in, filling the lungs *but only to a degree that is appropriate to the size of the space*. Breathe in as if you were filling your lungs with the air in the space. If it is a small room, take no more than a normal breath. If it is a cavernous hall, take a larger, longer breath. Then confidently and clearly speak your opening sentence. This breath prepares you psychologically for the amount of sound you are going to have to produce (whether or not there is a public address system is not the point). In addition it introduces a pause that is almost always of an appropriate length. It allows listeners to fix their attention, and it also provides a very helpful – if brief – moment of calm for the speaker.

Developing the voice cannot be taught in a book, any more than can riding a bicycle. An exhaustive and practical discussion of voice production and speech articulation cannot be given here.[7] Breathing from the diaphragm, resonating from the chest, projecting without shouting: these may seem like arcane techniques, yet they are the simple skills of the actor's and singer's craft. Of course, treatment of specific and individual problems requires the close attention of a professional speech therapist. But even if you do not suffer from noticeable problems or impediments (or have not yet been told about them), a few hours spent in a dedicated voice class can valuably serve a lifetime of ministry. Seek out such a class – if not now, then tomorrow. Some books have been recommended to make a start, in which case their exercises and activities, like the few given here, must be practised or they will have no effect whatsoever. No head knowledge will substitute for learning practically, ideally with a teacher, the correct way to produce a voice that is powerful, expressive, and flexible. Do it. Your ministry may depend upon it. Have I overstated that? I don't think so.

Is that all?

Of course not, any more than being able to tune your violin enables you perform a Mozart sonata. Furthermore, I would not leave you with impression that the voice is somehow an instrument separate from you, the player. It is linked in deep, deep ways both with who you are, and with what you are attempting to express. In any public speaking instance, while you are actually speaking, it will not do to give attention to the production of sound for more than few tiny instants, if at all. The exercises are given to strengthen, to protect, to extend the range, and to engrain good and effective habits. When good habits are second nature, then, and really only then can natural and effective public speaking begin.

8

Communication and communion

Geoffrey Stevenson

Communication enables communion. Our communication – at least until the advent of some computer-mediated universal cyber-church – is embodied. Yet we (Christian leaders and preachers) routinely act as if this were, at best, an inconvenience. Many mount pulpit steps and appear to wish they were somewhere else, and it is no wonder that so do many of their captive listeners.

How can the sermon be embodied, positively, respectfully and effectively? In this chapter we continue to look at aspects of sermon presentation or delivery, and what it means to embody – literally – the words that the preacher has so carefully and prayerfully crafted. This is not specifically about the kind of embodiment that concerns the preacher's integrity and personality, and how these validate or invalidate his speech. That is rightly the subject of another chapter (Chapter 4), as well as an excellent recently published book by David Day.[1] Here we are going to consider the physical means by which a sermon comes to be presented to a congregation and which invariably involve the face and body of the preacher.[2]

This is a larger part of the communication act than most speakers think. In 1971 Albert Mehrabian determined that in an act of face-to-face interpersonal communication, 55 per cent of all meaning was communicated through the body, 38 per cent through tone of voice, and 7 per cent by the actual words spoken.[3] Is that really true for preaching? OK, so in preaching to a group let us allow for a certain amount of filtering by the listener. Hearing a preacher they already know, they have probably learned to decode effectively and quickly the import of the vocal dynamics and tend to focus more substantially on the words, so the significance of the tone of voice may go down. Furthermore, they may not see all that much of the preacher, who will be standing some distance away, perhaps three-quarters hidden by a pulpit or lectern, and possibly even robed or otherwise obscured by trappings of liturgical practice. Perhaps then we might allow the words spoken a somewhat greater significance, but the challenge remains. We communicate through our bodies and faces, as well as through the rich language of vocal inflections (as mentioned in the last chapter). The body does not communicate ideas and concepts, but it does communicate emotion and attitude: whether we are excited or bored, 'on fire' or uncommitted, whether we believe what we say or are parroting something we think we are supposed to say. Our faces, bodies and the sound of our voices send out messages, and those messages are read with pretty fair accuracy by our listeners. We are speaking volumes with our bodies and faces. Three points:

1.   You cannot *not* have body language – you are always saying something, whether you stand to attention or move about restlessly, whether you keep your hands at your sides or wave them about with every phrase you speak.

2.   Your *preferred* body position and movements do say something about the kind of person you are. This directly relates to your credibility for the different things you say.

3.   If your words say one thing and your body another, people will believe what your body is saying, not the words.

So how can we ensure that our body language helps and does not hinder the reception of our words?

One thing to avoid is anything artificial or manners that have been imposed or grafted onto our natural personalities. The story has circulated for a while of a certain former US President who was renowned for being dull and wooden in front of the TV cameras. For a live broadcast (ironically, it was on the energy crisis), he was advised to animate his talk with gestures. There were stage directions in his speech, rolling up on the autocue before his eyes, and he gamely attempted to follow these while speaking. The result was jerky, unnatural and out of character, and it earned a chorus of ridicule from the press, who now dubbed him the Wooden Puppet.[4] The lesson should be clear: Speaking with animation and energy while appearing natural will not be mastered overnight. Furthermore, there are undoubtedly limits to the changes that can be achieved. In this area the individual is working at a deep level involving personality and identity, intimately interwoven as they are with our bodies. We are not pure, cerebral souls temporarily and somewhat inconveniently inhabiting a mortal body. We are bodies *and* mind *and* spirit, none of which can be separated from the other two without striking at the heart of who we are.

Changing habits

A trusted friend's feedback can accelerate the learning process in this sphere immensely.

Ask your friend to count the distracting mannerisms, or comment on the effectiveness of your new set of gestures or level of animation. (Maybe for the sake of your anxiety it would be good to limit the conversation to one or at most two things at a time!)

If there is a particular area that is worth correcting or improving, remember how habits are acquired or changed: gradually. Resolve to pay attention to just one habitual mannerism of gesture over the next half a dozen times that you are preaching. Amidst the pressure and the many calls on your concentration, this can only occupy a tiny proportion of your attention – just a few seconds of remembering not to rock back and forth, for example. Over time this project will succeed, but it is just one small project in the intentional development of the preacher.

The eyes have it

As social beings, we easily recognize and shrink from the extremes of human behaviour, and this is particularly true with the way people use their eyes. The ways the eyes behave are never without significance in human discourse. Long staring, or refusing to make any eye contact mark an individual as needing . . . shall we say, a little extra care and attention, or a wide berth. Most of the things we do with our eyes are unconscious. They are at the service of the complex demands of living and interacting. How long it is right to look into the eyes of another is finely judged by most of us, depending on the relationship, the social context and the physical situation. We all know (or should know) the difference between a look, a gaze and a stare, though they are measured in split seconds.

In Northern European cultures, it seems as if the *listener* has permission to look at a *speaker* for as long as he or she wishes, particularly if in a group of listeners. There is an observing, attentive quality to looking while listening, and it undoubtedly encourages the speaker. On the other hand, the *speaker* should not look at the listener for long periods, as this would be perceived as either intimidating or overly intimate. However, they should be making enough eye contact regularly with the listener to assure him implicitly that the message is personally directed at him. What many preachers fail to learn is that there are still rules that apply when speaking to groups, however large. The larger the group, the more permission the *listener* has to look or look away at will (or to fall asleep, as preachers continue to find). But the *speaker* still has a responsibility to make eye contact with each listener for a few significant seconds. They should not merely glance, or let their eyes dart around, as these tend to convey lack of conviction or integrity. Nor should they stare at one person, lest the moral force of the words being spoken be received as a form of religious abuse! As tempting as it is, the speaker should try not to favour the ones who give back encouraging smiles or who affirm in other ways.

Having learnt the difference between talking *to* and talking *at*, practise in your next sermon spending a couple of seconds engaging with each person as you speak. When the group is large, further away, or spread out in a large space, make eye contact with clusters rather than individuals.

What's in a smile?

Naturally I have no idea what kind of face you have: whether your smile is broad, frequently creasing your face from ear to ear, or a rare, thin-lipped affair that is only marked by a small upturn at the corners of your mouth. Do your eyebrows customarily travel several inches up and down between emotions of scowling and open-mouthed surprise? Or are they virtually immobile, allowed only the faintest lift to question silently something you have just heard or read? Are you so sure that when you are smiling on the inside, there is very much smile coming through on the outside? It may be worth checking with someone who knows you.

Now think of your place in the pulpit, or where you ordinarily preach. How far away are most of your listeners? Of course, this will depend completely on the building and the type of gathering. Now I do not, as I have said, wish to change your personality, even if I could. All I am suggesting is that there is an appropriate degree of *projection* of your face, an increase in the volume, as it were, just as there is for your voice if you are to convey to a group what you can easily convey in one-to-one conversation. Work with possible feelings of falsity and exaggeration, and make them the subject of conscious experiments. Eventually, let me assure you, it will feel natural to you, and look natural to your listeners.

We all have our characteristic facial gestures and grimaces, and most of the time we are unaware of the mechanisms that produce them, just as we are most of the time unaware of the effects they produce in others. But maybe this one time you could consider becoming as a child again and studying your expressions in a mirror.

What does 'surprise' look like on your face? Now exaggerate it. Try scowling in anger. Now exaggerate it, push the features to the extreme, with your fingertips if necessary. Finally make a huge grin at yourself, stretching the mouth wide and letting the jaw drop and the eyebrows rise up, while opening the eyes wide.

Next, away from the mirror, try some of these face exercises. The skin and muscles of the face are unlikely ever to do on the spur of the moment what they have never done previously through this kind of exercise, so think of this as expanding the range of expressiveness that is available to you when the occasion demands. They are also excellent as a kind of wake-up call for the face. For maximum benefit, you should go all out with these, and push yourself, and do the whole sequence. (You will probably *really* want to be alone when you try this, but it's not for me to say.) There is not a 'right' way to do these exercises, but there is a wrong way: half-heartedly. So may I encourage you to 'loosen up'?

Exercises for expressiveness

Stretch the features of the face as high and as wide as you can: raise the eyebrows, open the eyes wide, flare the nostrils, open the mouth, drop the jaw.

Then pull everything together – 'scrinch' your face as tightly as possible, as if you are trying to make your eyebrows and your chin meet at your nose.

Stretch wide again;

Scrinch together;

Wide; Together. Alternate another four times.

1. Make a chewing motion with your jaws, but keep your lips closed tight (tip: don't bite your tongue).

2. Yawn – a big yawn – but keep your lips together from start to finish.

3. Take a breath and say 'oooooooooooh', pushing your face and lips as far forward as you can.

4. Pull your head back and open your mouth horizontally wide and say 'aaaaaaaaaaah'.

   Lips forward: 'oooooooooooh'.

   Head back, 'aaaaaaaaaaah'; Forward: 'oooooooooh', Back: 'aaaaaaaaah'. Alternate, increasing speed: 'oooooooooooh – aaaaaaaaaaah' – 'oooooooooooh – aaaaaaaaaaah'.

5. Raise and drop the eyebrows eight times.

6. Pull the mouth wide open horizontally (don't move the jaw), and then relax, eight times.

   Next, eyebrows up and down four times, mouth wide, four times.

   Then, eyebrows twice, mouth twice, eyebrows twice, mouth twice, and finally quickly alternate: eyebrows – mouth, four times each.

7. Finally, turn to the mirror and make your exaggerated surprised, scowling and happy faces.

Now forget you ever did this last exercise (an actor would never try to put on a face to go with a sentiment). Go into your next preaching or public speaking event determined to reach out to your listeners with all that your have: your words of course, but also your voice, your face, your body. Some of the best public speaking advice I ever had was, 'Be yourself – only more so.' I only wish I could remember who said it.

All show and no tell?

Thomas Hardy wrote a gleefully satirical depiction of a preacher congratulating himself after a powerful pulpit performance, unaware that he was being watched by a parishioner, who saw him stand at a mirror

> . . . and re-enact at the vestry-glass
>
> Each pulpit gesture in deft dumb-show
>
> That had moved the congregation so.[5]

Such self-conscious sermon grandstanding is rare these days, for the style of public speaking in general has changed in many ways. However, some – such as the Wooden Puppet president mentioned earlier – can clearly do with more physical energy and bodily animation while they are speaking. A sermon preached in class that I listened to last month is fresh in my mind because of a simple gesture the preacher used to help an illustration. He was describing the location fix that 'satnav' makes possible, and he made an X with his arms in front of him to represent the point where the beams crossed. He was using it as a simile for two apparently conflicting understandings of God's judgement and God's mercy that can nevertheless give us a location fix in our lives. The gesture, repeated a couple of times later on, made the point instantly memorable, with the cross shape providing, of course, another layer of meaning.

It isn't necessary to find an action for every image in your sermon, nor indeed will there be one of such simple effectiveness every time you need it. But most public speaking would be improved with a judicious incorporation of hand and arm gestures to punctuate and underscore the speech. Of course, no one can prescribe or choreograph for you in this area. The process of improvement in this as in any kinaesthetic accomplishment begins with observing your own practice and noting what works in the practice of others.

There are two rules or habits that may be safely adopted by almost every public speaker, however:

1.   You should consciously resist vague or limp gestures whenever you catch yourself doing them. Stillness, with intensity and composure is seldom a fault.

2.   Any remaining gestures should (a) be definite, (b) look intentional and (c) be sparingly employed.

Gesture exercises

1.   Count the number and different types of gesture employed by a practised preacher or public speaker. How many seem intentional, and support the speech, and how many are vague, indeterminate, or seem unconnected with the meaning and emotional force of the words being spoken?

2.   As a game or exercise, practice gesturing while speaking to a friend. Standing a metre apart, firstly explain an activity, such as preparing the pet cat's dinner, while forcing yourself to keep your hands at your side, very still. Then explain another activity, such as what you have to do to reach your favourite view of countryside, while never letting your arms drop below your waist. Experiment with some large arm movements while talking, and listen to the feedback afterwards on how strange or natural your movements looked to your listener.

Filling the space

David Cunningham[6] once pointed out to me that 'church spaces make theological statements' by which he meant that the building in which we worship, and the way we use it, represent and often irresistibly convey theological interpretations and understandings of leadership, liturgy and ecclesiology.

For instance, rows and rows of fixed pews restricting individual movement and all facing the same way, towards the leadership who are at the front in position of control, convey many things to the sensitive observer. One is a strong distinction between clergy and laity. Another image is that of a bus driver and his or her passengers. The church is going somewhere, the laity are being taken on the journey, and it is being driven by the minister. There are sometimes even conductors to come round to take your fare.

When a seated and largely passive congregation face a dominating pulpit, the model is one of pedagogy: teaching and instruction and exposition are the practices best served by this arrangement. By contrast, when the church meets in a hall or large open space with an altar situated at the centre of concentric rings of seats, so that everyone is facing almost every one else, the performance aspects of an individual are reduced, while participative and egalitarian values are enhanced.[7]

All this is to say that preaching has to be done from some position or other, which may or may not be fixed, and it is done *to* (or better, with) a congregation who are situated in a particular space. The purpose of this brief section is to consider how that relationship is affected by the space.

Preaching from a fixed pulpit is by far the most common location in traditional church buildings, for obvious reasons to do with *audibility* and *sightlines*. As far as audibility is concerned, public address systems have made preaching from different positions possible. The use of wireless microphones further extends the options – though not without peril, as the occasional horror story attests, of the microphone being left on while unguarded comments are made in the vestry for the entire church to hear.

Sightlines are also less of an issue when coming out of the pulpit to preach. This is principally because churches are typically attended by far fewer worshippers than the buildings were designed for. Speaking from the chancel steps, or a platform at the front which may vary from a few centimetres to a metre high, works well in visual terms. Listeners can see much more of the speaker. In fact, in the case of preachers whose height does not match the 'design parameters' of the traditional pulpit, there is a real advantage to coming out to the front. So why do some persist in using a pulpit?

The symbolism of being 'six foot above contradiction' must not be underestimated. There is an understanding of the office of the preacher that benefits from the symbolic reinforcement of the significance of the word of God. This is well served by architectural elements that not only raise the preacher physically, but ennoble and virtually enthrone the preaching of the word. For a number of established as well as Free Church traditions, robes contribute and reinforce the belief that it is not the man or woman standing before us whom we are listening to, but God through an appointed mouthpiece.

In many churches the distinction between ordinary communication and being the mouthpiece of God is subtle, but exists in terminology and use of the space. On the one hand, the *sermon* can only be delivered by a robed and licensed minister speaking from the pulpit. On the other, an un-licensed person in 'street dress' and speaking from the same level as the congregation would be delivering an *address*. The reading of Scripture, done from a privileged but separate position, with a dedicated and elaborate lectern, is often termed a *lesson*. The reading from the

Gospels takes place with special acclamations (in some liturgical traditions) and may take place in the centre of the congregation. Depending on your tradition, these practices may seem fussy or full of symbolic significance, but they are not without theological meaning.

Take a moment to describe the theology and the effects on the participants of your space and how it is used for the ministry of the word.

Watching your back

Is the sun in your eyes as you preach? Try not to worry about it. It can be a distraction for you, but at least the congregation can probably see you extremely well.

Is the sun coming from behind you and shining in their eyes? Then do all and anything you can to curtain off the light or change your position.

Is your usual position for preaching in shadows or poorly lit? Seriously consider improving the lighting when the next opportunity (and funding) arises for a re-ordering or upgrade to the facilities. It may be a difficult case to argue, but remember the listeners, some of whom may struggle at the best of times to concentrate on the spoken words for a full 7, 17 or 47 minutes. Visual distractions may well be critical for them.

Exercise when in an empty church
Deliver the first 3 minutes of a recent sermon from 4 or 5 different positions in the church, imagining the congregation and the occasion as vividly as possible. Consider what happens to the 'sermon act' from each of those different positions, in terms of:

- its volume;

- its pace;

- its warmth;

- its authority.

Faith comes through hearing

A public address or PA system is a necessity in church today, for several reasons.

One is that a powerful bass or baritone voice, of the type best able to fill an average sized church or school hall, is not common to many men, and even less so for most women. A PA system frees a quieter woman's voice from being forced to project, with all the dangers noted in the last chapter. However it should still be noted that a PA system should not be seen as a substitute for elementary voice training that I have argued should be a part of every preacher's formation.

Secondly, good voice training and practice over a few years makes it possible to utilize a PA system for subtle expressiveness. With experience and practice a preacher becomes better able to control vocal dynamics, colouring his or her voice according to the material. The principal techniques are moving in to a fixed microphone for an intimate, softly spoken word, and pulling well back in order to raise the voice to make a more passionate kind of point.

Thirdly, a good PA system makes it far easier for inexperienced preachers to adopt a conversational tone of address when this is the register sought for the sermon being preached.

Finally, the most important reason for having a PA system is that it is the most usual way to incorporate a *hearing aid loop* into the worship space. This enables the church to comply with one of the requirements of the Disability Discrimination Act. Note that it is possible to fit inductive loop systems that do not require an amplification system. They will work with fixed, *boundary* microphones that pick up nearby voices, but far better results are obtained from microphones that are hand-held or that clip on to the speaker's clothing. These may, of course, be either wired or wireless. Specialist advice should be sought, or may be found through an Internet search on the keywords *church, disability discrimination act* and *hearing*.

So now you have the PA system. What about learning to use it? Increasing use of clip-on microphones is a blessing by and large, but there are two golden rules:

1. *Place the microphone carefully.* It must be close enough to the area on your body just below the collar bone in order to pick up the voice well, but absolutely beyond the danger of being rubbed, dislodged or knocked by clothing, jewellery, pectoral crosses etc.

2. In the case of a wireless microphone, *know how to switch it on and off*. This will need to be done inconspicuously, so you need to remember which way is which (especially when singing with the congregation, attempting a confidential conversation or going to the toilet!)

Good microphone technique with a fixed (hand-held or stand-mounted) microphone is a skill learned by singers and orators, and acquired principally by experience. Three basic techniques may be usefully explained here:

1. Find or take instruction on the *optimum distance* you should keep between your mouth and the head of the microphone. This may be as close as 1 cm, for microphones designed for singers in a band, or as far away as 15–20 cm for other kinds of microphones, and if the PA system has been set up properly for it. If you are too far away, either the microphone will not pick up your voice sufficiently, or the amplifier volume will have to be turned up so high that there is a risk of feedback or 'howl'. If you are too close, the volume will be too loud and the sound will distort and become unpleasant to listen to.

2. *Stay 'on mike'* especially when trying to maintain eye contact with different sections of the congregation. Do this by keeping your mouth directed towards the microphone and turning your head and upper body around the head or business end of the microphone, all the while maintaining the optimum distance you have already established. This may mean you are speaking at the side of the head of the microphone, but that's OK, as most microphones are as sensitive at a 45-degree or even 60-degree angle as they are from straight on.

3. Learn to *avoid 'popping'* the microphone, which occurs when so-called 'plosive' consonant sounds such as 'p' and 't' direct the air from your lips straight at the sensitive pickup within the microphone. Popping is avoided by offsetting the mouth from the microphone, and aiming slightly over or under (or if necessary to the side).

All of these rules are learned through experimentation with the equipment, and this should be undertaken whenever possible when facing a new PA system. When you are due to speak in an unfamiliar church building, ask to try the microphone and its PA system without the congregation for a few minutes.

When the building is 'your own,' an hour or two with the PA, trying it out in the empty hall or church, is crucial to being able to use it well.

Finally, in a very large building with a powerful PA system and especially where there is a difficult acoustic, the preacher is completely at the mercy of the operator. Make sure to befriend them. Sometimes in churches there are volunteers in charge who are, shall we say, less skilled than is desirable. Extreme charm and advanced diplomacy are necessary. Personally, I would say that allowing the PA system to feedback or howl during public worship does not always require an ASBO be slapped on the offender, but it comes close. At any rate, try to establish a working understanding. Your listeners are worth the effort.

PowerPoint™ – or pointless technology?

Because PowerPoint™ is the predominant computer-based presentation software, widely available to schools, churches and businesses, it has become not only a generic word (like 'hoover') but also the standard for controlling the projection of visual images in business and education environments. However, there are alternatives less rooted in the fact-based and concept-oriented world of business presentations.[8] Not only does the use of these make a useful protest against the hegemony of a certain global company, but they also carry with them basic usage practices that are friendlier to the kinds of preaching that do not seek solely to present concepts and precepts and ideas distilled from consideration of a biblical text. I wish that something like 'digital visual projection' (while more of a mouthful) or 'DVP' became the common parlance for the use of a data projector and screen, controlled by software enabling text, image and video to be presented.

Of course, the use of visual projection technology in preaching is a rhetorical issue, concerned with how God's word is presented and received. This makes it is a deeply theological issue, not least in the area of the use of image.[9]

There are, of course, many, many technical issues involved in using this technology, such as controlling the software, finding sources for images, observing legal and copyright considerations, positioning and hooking up the hardware and, most importantly, getting it all to work reliably and with the minimum of fuss during worship and a sermon. Most of those are beyond the scope of this book, not least because there are so many products, and so many new ones appearing every day, that no text like this can hope to be comprehensive and up-to-date. Manuals and training programmes are available, however, for such areas, and all I can say is, make use of them before disaster happens!

It is possible and even desirable for a preacher with many other pastoral responsibilities to work with others on the production and projection of visual images to go with the sermon. Ideally, such colleagues will be master of many of the technical aspects of the software and the hardware in order to create the sequence of images and to present them seamlessly. For those who are technologically blessed and persistent enough to try it, alone or with others, there is one vital principle that will help to guide early experiments: *Focus the viewer's attention*.

The preacher's mid-sermon relationship with the congregation is very easily compromised or crippled by a screenful of 'eye candy'. Once a group of listeners is given a screen to watch, such is the appeal of tele-visual information that good eye contact with the listeners is impossible to maintain. In McLuhan's terms, the communication moves from cool to hot, and the listener has less to do to stay involved. Therefore the *focus of attention* must be controlled and directed by the preacher/presenter. There are different styles or stages:

1. When there is the slightest possibility, from the congregation's point of view, of something new on the screen, then that is where the focus of attention will be. You may assume that most people, most of the time will be looking at or frequently glancing at the screen, and that any significant gestures or expressions that you make will be missed by most people. Moreover a changing screen, with new words or pictures appearing every second or two, will seriously distract most listeners from your spoken words.

2. When the screen remains unchanging, showing, for instance an image or a set of words, some bullet points or a quotation, it will take a few moments for this to sink in, but eventually listeners will settle down to spending some time looking at you, and some at the screen. This is very much dependent on individual preferences and their liking for visual information. Those whose imagination is stimulated more by pictures and less by ideas or words will appreciate having a projected image to contemplate while listening to your voice.

3. When it is particularly important that the listener pay attention to what is on the screen, this should be emphasized by you looking at the screen, or at least more at the screen than at your notes or the congregation. You may keep silent, if there is a video with soundtrack or if you want the pictures to speak with maximum impact and freedom for the viewers to respond in their own ways. If there is a way of interpreting the images that you wish to share, then that may be done either in an explanation *before* the video or image sequence, or simultaneously. The skill to be developed is to work with the pictures, not against them.

4. When it is important that you as speaker are the focus of attention, and the beginning and end of the sermon are two such times in particular, there are two things to do:

   a. Let the screen fade to black, and do not project any words or images for a time.
   b. Make sure you establish good eye contact with the listeners.

   In these ways and others you are directing the focus of attention. It can be done subtly, or very overtly, but it should not be neglected out of carelessness. Nor should it be seen as manipulative. It is simply a feature of a well-developed communication skill set, and a vital component of an effective act of delivery.

When you are next able to use a projector of some kind while preaching, experiment with the incorporation of just one image or quotation per major section of the sermon. Let the screen go black, or remain empty, for other significant periods in the sermon, while you work with your words to create pictures for the listener. (Remember, less is more.)

Communication is an embodied event. While it can take years to master all the aspects of effective public speaking, we should take enormous comfort from this truth: so many are the complex and sometimes mysterious ways of God and of humanity, loved by him and created in his image, that the act of preaching will never be reduced to a set of techniques. There is an unpredictable glory in God's self-revelation, and a wonder in the way fallen and corruptible vessels such as ourselves contain and transmit that revelation. We study techniques, we strive to be better at the craft of preaching, we are appalled or disappointed at our failures, and yet we rejoice in the inexplicable and uncontrollable presence of God in the communion created through communication.

9

Preaching in community – the sermon as expression of the congregation

Geoffrey Stevenson

What happens if we view preaching as a congregational activity – before, during and after what we have on occasion called the sermon-event?

Before the event, there is the wider context of the sermon: the culture surrounding the church and preacher, the social and economic make-up of the community, the congregation's self-understanding, its needs and expectations. Taking these into account will mean that the sermon is (if only in part) an expression of the congregation. I will explore other ways that the sermon can be shaped by the congregation before it is preached.

During the sermon, while there may be ordinarily only one mouthpiece,[1] there are multiple hearers making multiple meanings out of the poor, bare words of the preacher. Again, we will look at what kind of listening is going on. Can the preacher help the listeners? Can the listeners help the preacher?

After the sermon, its multiple meanings are worked out in the body of Christ: corporately, as well as in the lives of individuals conscious of their relationship with God. Individuals will respond *surprisingly* differently from one another. These multiple meanings are applied and brought to life in multiple ways by the Holy Spirit, but are there practical ways the preacher can enhance this?

Before the sermon: *the voice of the congregation*

I want to commend this simple description of preachers by Jürgen Moltmann: 'They come from God's people, stand up in front of God's people, and act in God's name.'[2] If this were referring to leadership, 'to come from God's people' could be and has been interpreted in many ways, from arguments for lay presidency at communion to the distinct (and even 'ontological') calling out from the community of a priest in such as way as to mark him or her for life. Referring to preaching, however, the sermon is an 'expression of the congregation' in so far as the preacher has correctly heard and understood God's particular purpose and intent for *this* sermon at *this* time, in *this* place and for *these* people. This extreme particularity makes preaching more like prophecy than it is like teaching or public leadership. In so far as it is (in this narrow sense) prophetic, it is the application of the word by the Holy Spirit. It is also more of a *gift* than an *office*.[3] This gives preaching, as Oliver O'Donovan says, 'a disturbing open-endedness'.

As well as the listening for God commended in Chapter 4, active and intentional listening to the congregation will also be a very significant way of hearing God's voice, of 'feeling his heartbeat'.

The preacher with the heart of a pastor already does this in preparation, to a greater or lesser degree, knowing the spoken and unspoken needs of the church. He or she will not be preaching *at* individuals, but speaking words that are relevant to their kinds of situations, wrestling with their demons, exploring their doubts, articulating (if not always answering) their questions. Pastoral visiting and numerous other forms of pastoral contact must be allowed to shape the message of the sermon.

Even in the study, during preparation, it can be helpful to spend time remembering, imagining, visualizing the people who will be hearing the sermon when it comes to be preached. How will so-and-so hear this word, deep in the grief of her widowhood? What will the young parents, struggling with kids, jobs, mortgages and sometimes each other take away from the sermon? Of course, the sermon will not be preached to any of them directly, and with even the best will and a lengthy sermon slot, it is impossible to address directly the life-situations of all your listeners. The aim of this prayerful exercise of the imagination is to fire and inspire sermon preparation, and to give the developing sermon a reality check.

Another form of listening recognizes that it's not just what people say to the minister, but what they watch, read and listen to. Why draw all your metaphors from cricket and your news references from the *Today* programme when your listeners follow football (or no sport at all) and watch Breakfast TV? A small questionnaire, an audit of your congregation's media consumption, to be filled in anonymously, could be an eye-opener for you. Then revisit the section in Chapter 4 on 'understanding contemporary culture'. Be sure you conduct a little survey of your own habits and preferences as well.[4]

Another suggestion is to hold a preaching Bible study group, once or twice per month. Ideally this is where you bring the fruits of some exegetical study to share (recognizing that not many, I suspect, will come wanting to know more about the

Amalekites), and they bring a willingness to suggest connections between the reading and their family, work and personal concerns.

One preacher's Bible listening group was looking at the incident where Jesus is left behind by his parents (Luke 2.41-52), but instead of jumping into the thicket of Luke's theological intentions and the vast wisdom of many commentators, they were invited to share personal stories of having been left behind as a child, or having lost a child. Needless to say the stories were riveting and emotionally powerful. None related directly to the text. Hearing them all, the preacher was not necessarily any closer to a 'preachable point' coming out of the passage. But the preacher did have a rich collection of narrative and imagistic resources available to incorporate into a sermon that would invite listeners into the story and explore parenting and loss, both divine and human. Of course, he needed permission to use suitably disguised versions of some of the stories that had been told. Also, too much magpie behaviour like this would undoubtedly lead to feelings in the group that they were being used, so other times the result for the preacher would be an unusual angle or unexpected insight coming from the interaction between text and listeners.

John S. McClure takes this a step further in a strategy he calls collaborative preaching. 'In collaborative preaching, a revolving, expanding "sermon roundtable" is established in the congregation. The pastor and a small, periodically changing group of church members meet to discuss the concerns and ministries of the church in light of the biblical texts to be preached on Sunday morning.'[5]

These are all ways in which the community has an opportunity to be part of the sermon before it is preached. What is the congregation's role during the sermon?

During the sermon

Modes of speaking

As the old preacher's joke goes, 'My job is to speak and yours is to listen, and if you finish your job before I finish mine, please stay seated.' However, to enable listening there is some extra work to be done – there must be a common language and shared modes of speaking.

Here are some interesting results of informal surveys on sermon retention in the US:

- 51 per cent remembered one point, but it was never the main one.

- 10 per cent remembered more than one point, but the more points they remembered, the more points they invented.

- 37 per cent could not remember any points at all.[6]

It is easy to back up these findings with studies from the world of educational theory that demonstrate the weakness of the expository lecture style as a means of effective teaching,[7] but this is not a counsel of despair. It is worth recalling that remembering the points of a sermon is not the whole point of a sermon, particularly when the sermon is viewed as a moment of encounter or a space for the listener to make their own connections and transactions with God. Furthermore, the effect of preaching may often be likened more to sustenance than the building of an edifice of knowledge. I cannot remember any but a tiny number of the meals my mother prepared for me, but I certainly know I was fed and that I grew because of them.

Where teaching is an important part of a sermon or series of sermons, there is an argument, from those figures, for working to make the point more accessible, more memorable. This means paying attention to the different learning styles. These have been characterized in many ways recently in educational theory and schemata. One approach that I have found particularly useful and easy to grasp is from David Schlafer – he distinguishes three basic modes of communication throughout Scripture – images, narratives and argument:[8]

- *Images* are simply pictures formed through words – the stuff of poetry and lyrical writing, e.g. 'sheltering under the shadow of his wings'.

- *Narratives* need no examples, for all can see the Bible's pre-eminent mode of narrative and storytelling.

- *Argument* too, features strongly in biblical as well as sermonic communication, for it is where didactic explanation, a presentation of principle, a law or concept is brought forth.

There is nothing intrinsically sacred about these three – they are common modes of communication. Yet Schlafer argues: 'it is always through a combination of these that God reveals what God wishes human beings to understand'.[9] He therefore recommends sermonic strategies that seek similarly to employ all three. It is worth beginning by asking about the communication patterns that you customarily employ.

> Do you identify yourself primarily as a poet, a storyteller or an essay-writer? No preacher is exclusively a poet, storyteller or essayist, of course; effective preachers regularly use elements of each in all of their sermons. But most preachers have voice which is centred more in one mode of discourse than another.[10]

Earlier we looked at being storytellers and imagers, so I will not labour the point. My reason for bringing this out here is that people do tend to prefer, engage with, or respond to, one or another mode more strongly than the others. For example, what I remember most readily from the last sermon I heard is an image of a little boy leading a grown man by the hand. It was in the context of a story, the details of which are coming back to me as I try to recall. And in due course I daresay I will remember the point that was being illustrated by the story. But it was the image that hooked me, that stayed with me, that resonates with me emotionally, and in so doing is forming and shaping my understanding – or better, my appropriation into my life of the message. In contrast, others fasten most easily on to argument, and for them the images and stories may be like so much decoration. You will have your own preference, and your first job is to identify that.

For investigation

1. Scan a fair sampling of your sermons and see which predominates: argument, image or story, and by how much.

2. Try to determine what your listeners prefer. You can do this through casual conversation and informal polls. Ask them what they remember several hours, or two days, or a week after a sermon. Was it a picture that they formed in their minds from your words? Was it a story that was used to illustrate a point? Was it an idea or concept or truth, and if so, can you determine whether it was grasped and remembered because it had been persuasively argued for, or stated and then given rhetorical weight by repetition, or story, or image?

In these ways preaching can be structured, your speech can be formed so as to help listeners rather than hinder them.

Modes of listening

Some preachers need to learn to become storytellers, but some congregations need to learn to become story *listeners*. There is an African proverb well known among the professional storytelling community. It says: 'There are ears that have the power to open mouths'. But doesn't everybody love a good story? Surely the problem is too many preachers who have no idea what a good story is, or how to tell one. However, it isn't all down to the preacher. Congregations frequently come to church without any expectation that the story will speak to them. Another way of describing this expectation is *spiritual hunger*. A congregation needs to be encouraged to admit to and to own this hunger. It's about wanting to know and love God more closely, learning what it is to live the Christian life creatively – radically – dangerously. It is about approaching all our worship gatherings with ears that are open to the smallest whisper that may be heard through sacrament, worship, prayer, and yes, even preaching.

So, from time to time it is necessary in most churches to re-visit some of the basics of the practices of worship as well as the tenets of the faith. Just as teaching about worship in a series of sermons can be liberating for a congregation, so too some congregations might benefit from a sermon or two on listening to sermons. Maybe a respectful reminder or small challenge is in order – are we listening when Scripture is read? Are people expecting to hear something besides the words and what we usually, typically understand by them? When the preacher stands up to speak are we expecting to hear something that will make a difference to our lives: a word of challenge, or comfort, or inspiration, something to give us hope or direction or correction, something of which we can truly and honestly say, 'God has spoken'?

Anyone over 50 knows the question, 'Where you when you first heard of President Kennedy's assassination in 1963?' The novelist David Lodge, in the introduction to one of his books tells where he was: in a theatre watching the performance of a satirical revue he had helped write. In one sketch, a character was holding a transistor radio to his ear. It seems the actor playing the part always tuned in to a real broadcast. Suddenly came the announcement that President Kennedy had been shot. The actor quickly switched it off, but it was too late. The audience had heard. Reality had interrupted stage comedy.

For some believers, worship, prayer and Scripture are something of a nonchalant charade. They don't expect anything significant to happen. If suddenly God's reality were to break through they might be shocked.

High expectation is the key to many a good sermon, listening for the word that God longs to speak. It may be a word to give meaning to life. It may be a word to help make sense of living in a society that seems seriously to have lost its way. It may be a word to give hope, to know that in the pain of illness or grief there is a God who cares, who draws alongside in comfort or reassurance, able to give a light in the darkness, a drop of water to parched lips, an embrace in the loneliness.

Without expectation, without hunger, listeners will be unlikely to be in a position to receive. There may be something in this description of preachers attributed to Martin Luther: 'We are all mere beggars telling other beggars where to find bread.'

After the sermon – enacting the word together

Sadly, there are usually only two kinds of congregational feedback – both rather discouraging. One is a succession of 'Nice sermon, vicar' or 'I enjoyed your word' (depending on your tradition) comments at the door. These are well meant, but seldom believable and of no help at all the preacher seeking formative criticism. The other kind of feedback will be from the person who is delighted or moved to tell you something that they heard from God through the sermon. As you listen you realize that it has absolutely no logical connection with anything you remember saying. This response is not to be despised or derided, for the Holy Spirit is (thankfully) often at work despite our efforts. But again, it is not much help when looking to improve your preaching.[11]

I asked the New Testament professor James D. G. Dunn, who is also an active and well-respected Methodist preacher, to write for a book I was editing on how he developed as a preacher. This is what he said about working with the congregation:

> Occasionally I have experimented with congregational feedback and discussion of the sermon as part of the service, but this has rarely been very practicable. Here too I am influenced by Paul who never saw the delivery of a word from God as an act in itself but insisted that some within the congregation, or the congregation itself, should exercise discernment as to the significance and bearing of what had been said and as part of the congregation's gathering for worship (1 Corinthians 14.29; 1 Thessalonians 5.19-22). I still wish we could devise service structures where such further discussion could be possible. In the same way I have been glad occasionally to be able to take part in some team planning of services and to pre-discuss the sermon. Paul's vision of the congregation operating as the body of Christ (Romans 12.6-8; 1 Corinthians 12) has always thrilled and challenged me, with all sharing in ministry (a much broader, more profound concept of ministry) in mutual interdependence, and grace being corporately channelled to the whole rather than being overly (or exclusively) dependent on the insight and preparation of one individual.[12]

There are very good reasons for working with the sermon listeners, before and after the event. Why is it so difficult to initiate conversation and to keep the ball rolling? It requires commitment from the minister and the congregation, but it also depends a bit on chemistry and how the preacher is able to motivate others to a team effort. It also takes time, and ultimately may be a matter of priority. How much of a priority is it to listen to and to proclaim the word of God?

Finally, it is the case that technology can sometimes perfect an idea: 'When God's voice is heard'[13] is an example of a weblog that invites the preacher's readers to 'engage with scripture in community' by posting comments on the scripture readings and the preacher's initial thoughts for upcoming sermons. It does not need me to say how culturally significant the Internet is becoming in our society, and indeed so many are so in thrall to so many passing phenomena that it is very difficult to judge their long-term impact. However, it is certain that our concepts of communication, community, intimacy, self-disclosure, relationships and sharing are being altered by large-scale participation in online experiences, from simple email to elaborate social networking sites.

Once the 'online cyber-church' was a ridiculous idea. We were assured that God favoured face-to-face relationships. But it seems that before long we will have to develop our theologies of Church, liturgy and worship to understand those who participate in the Body of Christ fully, emotionally, interactively and yet mediated through a screen and keyboard. In the churches of this cyber wild west there will be some form of preaching: let those who have ears to hear, eyes to read, a mouse and a keyboard pay attention to what God is doing and the new wineskins that may be used.

To finish, allow me to redress the balance a little, to counter any impression that it is always the educated and superior preacher who has 'got it' and the listeners are the ones who haven't. Sometimes when listening to a preacher who is not very focused and well prepared, it is possible to discern, as Oliver O'Donovan says, 'the sermon that ought to have been preached that day'. Our congregations are graced, sometimes liberally, with Christians who have maturity, wisdom and experience, and even occasionally a good deal of biblical literacy and theological expertise beyond that of the young preacher. My advice is, try not to be intimidated when you see the face and recall that fact, three minutes into your sermon. Call to mind instead that it is the chief responsibility and pleasure of all present to hear and receive the word of the Lord. And remember that you are all in it together.

10

Preaching in a mission-conscious Church

Stephen Wright

In this last chapter we want to look ahead and comment briefly on four ways in which the form of preaching is evolving in response to the Church's renewed consciousness of being a missionary body. In various settings, the monologue sermon is mutating into interactive discussion; or the 'preacher' is taking on the role of 'motivator for mission'; or the whole service is being turned inside-out to become more 'seeker-friendly'; or the power of the image is challenging the hegemony of the word. Indeed, there may be a heady mixture of more than one of these developments (and no doubt others!).[1] We'll then stand back and ask what it is about 'preaching' which can and should endure through all these evolutions.

One voice bad, many voices good?

One of the fundamental features of the kinds of preaching described in Chapter 2 is that though they are part of corporate worship, normally just one person speaks. The only ones in which there is regularly some concession to active dialogue are (some) 'revivalist' preaching, and 'all-age' preaching. Even here, the single 'preacher' remains strongly in control.

Some have argued, however, that multi-voiced forms of preaching better express the dynamic forms of communication used by Jesus and the Early Church. Such forms are also seen as being more appropriate for a Church seeking to shed an outmoded, authoritarian manner linked to its 'Christendom' past, and more effective as 'teaching'.[2] Drama itself, with its undoubted power to move hearts and provoke thought, may be included under this heading. Furthermore, where the Church in its mission is breaking out of the structure of formal 'congregational' gatherings, and meeting in cell groups, pubs or cafés,[3] then it is natural that the formality of the 'sermon' should be abandoned. 'Preaching' starts to shade into 'discussion'.

Those who argue for some kind of interactive 'preaching' are not disputing the necessity of the gospel message being passed on. Indeed, it is interesting to see the strong links with the traditional types:

- Tim Stratford, based on his experience as vicar of the Good Shepherd, a large outer estate parish in the diocese of Liverpool, argues for an interactive model that clearly falls within the 'liturgical preaching' framework, allowing members of the congregation more of an active role in a 'sermon' conceived as part of a carefully planned journey of worship.[4]

- Educators David Norrington and Stuart Murray are clearly concerned with 'teaching', the passing on of biblical and doctrinal truth; their dispute with traditional preaching is whether the monologue is the best means.[5]

- The material about Jesus' own style of dialogue and interaction with people highlighted by Jeremy Thomson, Course Director of the Oasis Youth Work and Ministry Course, is particularly suggestive for 'apologetics', in which, it could be argued, some active engagement with our interlocutors is essential to an effective defence of the faith.[6]

Again, context is, of course, crucial. The informal meeting in the pub and the large Eucharist or teaching service call for very different styles of 'preaching'. Where there is interaction in the latter kind of event, it is most helpful for all concerned if it is carefully managed. This is not manipulation, but the decent ordering of a public event. On the other hand, if 'preaching' in the more informal settings did not include a healthy element of genuinely open-ended dialogue, there would be something seriously wrong!

From proclamation to mission-management

The awareness that the Church is in a 'mission' situation may lead directly to a notion of the purpose of preaching as 'mission-management' or 'mission-motivation'. The preacher is seen basically as the leader galvanizing the team for action.

Leadership is necessary for any human organization. In the Church, Jesus the servant is our pattern (Luke 22.24-30); but the ideal of service does not imply the absence of leadership roles and skills – they are gifts in Christ's body (Romans 12.8). However, it is interesting to see how far-reaching the shift is when the kinds of preaching described in Chapter 2 turn into exercises of leadership. The shift may be quite subtle; indeed it may not be immediately noticeable to congregations, especially those used to expository or revivalist preaching, which have regularly involved a direct challenge to the listeners. But when the aim of the preaching moves from being an attempt to convey God's word of grace for *all* people, to being an attempt to mobilize *these* people in accordance with a specific 'vision' or 'mission' which the leaders (or the church as a whole) believe they have received from God, an important shift has indeed taken place.

Michael Quicke makes a good case for the importance of 'full-blooded' preaching which refuses to stick to bland generalities and is earthed in the practical realities of the Church's local mission.[7] So, the church leaders have felt it right to start an after school club for kids, but it needs helpers: you then preach about the importance of 'letting the children come to Jesus'. Or the church has felt led to open its doors to the homeless: so you preach about Jesus' call to be compassionate to the outcast. Or the church has great plans for outreach, but has a shortfall against its annual budget: so you preach a sermon on giving based on 2 Corinthians 8 and 9. More traditional preaching of any of the types will have also dealt with these things. The difference is that in 'mission-management' mode, the preaching is overtly planned and focused on getting the congregation to do things. In the traditional types, this kind of motivation will be seen as a desirable side-effect, but there will usually be more caution about driving forward a particular agenda.

'Mission-management' preaching has links with the 'purpose-driven church' movement led by Rick Warren in the USA. Indeed, in contemporary Church parlance, 'mission' is often simply a metaphor for 'purpose'. We are not 'sent' anywhere far in a physical sense. But we see ourselves as 'people with a purpose'. Such self-awareness among Christians is to be welcomed. And we have explored earlier the value of integrating preaching with a deep pastoral awareness of the specific situation of the hearers.

However, the means of discerning more specific purposes of God for particular Christian groups or individuals are more controversial. There is the danger on the one hand of arrogant power-play masquerading as spiritual wisdom, and on the other hand of adopting the management techniques of big corporations, which may owe far more to the 'functional atheism' of technological modernity than to authentic Christianity. It is interesting to observe how many secular bodies have stolen the Church's clothes by adopting the language of 'mission' in their 'mission statements', and how the churches have stolen it back again, only to use it with its new, secular colouring. 'Purpose-driven preaching' therefore always needs to ask itself whose purpose is really in the driving seat.

Note too what such preaching 'says' about the congregations where it happens. It marks them out as specific groupings or organizations rather than a motley (but therefore representative) collection of humanity as a whole. This means that such preaching may reinforce a sense of 'us' and 'them', and may be more difficult for the 'outsider' or casual visitor to relate to. It is all about how 'we' can fulfil 'our' mission more effectively. It is not about how God calls and blesses anyone at all, whether 'us' or 'them'. 'Preaching' is no longer a representative act, one in which humanity as a whole is addressed by the gospel as a whole.

To say that this kind of 'leadership' preaching is no longer 'representative' preaching is not, in itself, to dismiss its value. Perhaps in some settings it is exactly what a congregation needs. It is to point out that in a fundamental sense it differs from the traditional types outlined earlier. It is also to put the question to preachers: are you simply colluding with the less-than-holy institution that you serve, in its plans and projects, or are you ready to subvert it and them where necessary in the name of the always-bigger truth – God himself and his good news?

From in-house talk to seeker sensitivity

A further development in preaching arising from the Church's mission-consciousness stems from the Willow Creek Church in the USA, which pioneered 'seeker services' especially tailored to the 'unchurched'. Bill Hybels has been the key figure here. The aim was to meet the interested 'outsider' more on his or her own territory than the Church's. Rather than inviting such people to church services where they would hear a lot of unfamiliar religious jargon and perhaps be embarrassed by being asked to say or sing things they didn't understand or believe, the idea is to offer 'services' which essentially consist of a talk on some contemporary life-issues – work, family, money and the like – from a Christian perspective. In comfortable, non-threatening surroundings, the uncommitted are able to explore the relevance of Christian faith. In time, many have through this route become committed, worshipping members of the Church.

'Seeker' preaching is clearly a kind of 'apologetic' preaching. What marks the Willow Creek movement out as a fresh and distinctive approach to preaching, however, is the radical way in which the traditional church's priorities are turned on their head. Rather than having 'guest' or 'evangelistic' services as occasional events, Willow Creek made 'seeker' services central. Services of worship for the committed continued, but they were no longer the pivot around which the life of the church revolved.

Willow Creek represents an important and creative response to the situation of declining church membership. It deliberately takes the word beyond the walls of worship. It is truly missionary in its outward-looking concern. The possible critique comes, interestingly, from two sides.

On the one hand, some would see the kind of preaching practised in 'seeker services' as too like some more traditional kinds: in other words, a public monologue with still too much of the authoritarian and/or rationalist whiff of 'we have the answer'. On the other hand, the divorce between services for 'seekers' and those for 'the committed' may be problematic. It could reinforce the sense of 'us' and 'them', and could undermine the sense that the gospel needs to go on being heard by believers. Nonetheless, the attempt of Willow Creek to address the real-life problems and questions faced by people in their particular cultural setting is courageous and represents the boundary-breaking, incarnational thrust of the gospel. All groups of Christians should ask themselves how best to follow through this thrust for the cultures in which they live. In a world where such cultures increasingly jostle alongside each other in bewildering variety, this is a challenge, but one which the people of Pentecost are surely equipped to undertake!

From word to image

The final shift in preaching in response to the missionary demands of the time may appear at first sight the most far-reaching. Sometimes one senses a fundamental questioning of the very adequacy of the spoken word.

This does not, of course, usually mean that words are dispensed with altogether. There are not many within the Church who would argue for a policy of complete silence! (Quakers, who appreciate more than most the value of silence in worship, are vocal in speaking out for justice and peace!) It is rather that the power of image as a supplement to word is being rediscovered. Some would go further, saying that images are not only powerful, but indispensable. In a society often described as 'image-saturated', so the thought runs, preaching which is only 'words' will no longer do. Many creative means of communication are being explored, often harnessing the latest electronic technology, and we have touched on this in Chapter 8.

In fact, of course, image has accompanied word through much of Christian history. For many Christians, icons have been an important element of worship since early times. Gregory of Nyssa called icons 'silent Scriptures that speak from the walls'.[8] Stained-glass windows told the stories of the Bible for those who could not read. Indeed, not just visual symbols, but symbols appealing to all the senses have been a part of the communicative medium of faith from the start. Taste, touch and even smell have been a regular part of sacramental worship, as well as hearing and sight. Practitioners of liturgical preaching might argue, indeed, that their preaching has always been surrounded by plenty of visual and symbolic elements, and that these new developments are simply catching up with them![9] In one sense, too, the greater incorporation of the visual and symbolic in preaching is just an extension of the blending of 'sermon' with 'service' that we noted as a tendency in revivalist and 'all-age' preaching. It is another way in which the preaching may be bound together more tightly with the whole occasion.

The incorporation of more visual and symbolic elements into the preaching of churches where previously 'word' reigned supreme might therefore be seen as just the enhancement of traditional forms of preaching, rather than something radically new. It marks a return from a too-narrow intellectual approach to passing on the faith, to one that appeals to the whole person in a more rounded way. As we saw in Chapter 1, modern Western culture has been closely linked to Protestantism with its strong emphasis on the word and words (inextricably bound up with the invention and development of printing). Some observers are now asking whether this has led to an imbalance both culturally and spiritually. The cultural shift of so-called 'postmodernity' reflects a re-awakening of the spiritual and the sensory in human desire and experience. A totally word-oriented Church barren of sensory elements may be ill-equipped to respond to these yearnings. Technology, of course, opens up many possibilities for a broader approach that have never been available before.

There is, though, a deeper dynamic at work too. Some of the more radical recent philosophers have taught us to be suspicious of words as tools of power – they appear to be so innocent and objective, yet they are always bound up with some human agenda that may not be immediately obvious. In this climate, preaching is as much a suspect as any other form of speech.

Yet we cannot do without words, and they continue to serve us well in our everyday life. Even the radical philosophers can't do without them! On their own, images and other non-verbal symbols may be even more open to manipulation and misuse than words are. Just downplaying words is not going to overcome any problems of trust that people may have with the Church's communication.

There is a lot, after all, to be said for the traditional balance between word and sacrament. Words give clarity and direction to symbols. Symbols remind us that words can never completely capture the truth, but that we are grasped by the truth as we open ourselves to it on all levels of our personality, not just the intellect. Moreover, words themselves can be used in a rich multiplicity of ways. As we have seen, many recent preaching authors point to the value of the poetic, the artistic, the narrative in preaching.[10] Although different preachers will be drawn to different styles, and varied settings will call for variety in approach, an awareness of the riches of verbal language goes a long way to countering the notion that words are 'tired'. Meanwhile, many preachers are experimenting in creative ways with the use of images and other symbols to enhance communication of the message.

Evaluating the shifts

What is at stake in these changing conceptions of preaching? There is no dispute among Christians that the gospel goes on needing to be communicated. But what is it about *preaching* that can, and should, endure in and through this kaleidoscope of shifting forms? Perhaps there are four elements in particular to be treasured and guarded.

The first is *the gift of words*. Words are precious tools: tokens of self-giving, of relationship. The issue is not whether we use them, but *how* we use them. They are devalued if used thoughtlessly. Their power is diminished if they are not used with attention to their surrounding context, and in creative combination with silence and symbol. There are many possibilities here, and those responsible for preaching surely have liberty to explore them together.

The second is *the maintenance of the centre*. 'Maintenance' has almost become a dirty word in church circles, contrasted with 'mission'. Contemporary missiological thinking is surely right to emphasize the need to see mission as an activity of God that far transcends the doings of the institutional Church, and to encourage Christians to speak and embody the message in whatever settings in society they have access to. The corollary of this is that we are surely right to see preaching as only a part – perhaps often quite a small part – of the whole missionary enterprise.

However, as the disciples returned to Jesus after their missionary forays (Mark 6.30), so Christians today need to meet together, to be refreshed, to be continually reminded of the good news which gives us our identity and mission, with all its breathtaking implications. Preaching, in whatever form, surely has a key place in this act of remembering. This is what we have described as the importance of tradition.

Like any organization, the Church needs a strong centre: a shop window, as it were, guaranteeing the authenticity of the message being shared by its representatives all through society. Those working mainly in the shop-window should not assume that their work is all there is to it, any more than those beavering away in their networks should assume that they can survive without the central focus. And within that central focus of public worship, preaching plays its part. Although inevitably preachers are fallible representatives, that public event can and should be a litmus test for the genuineness of our many missionary activities. Manning the centre may not always be as exciting as serving on the front line. It does not need to be. That does not diminish its importance.

The third is *the claiming of public space*. One of the main trends within society over the last three hundred years has been the 'privatization' of religion, including Christianity.[11] Preaching, as some form of *public* affirmation of the Christian story, is a fundamental act of resistance to this trend. The very event of preaching challenges the notion that faith is merely something to be explored in informal, private settings by consenting adults. We may feel that the 'public space' being claimed by a sermon is a very limited one, but we should not underestimate the significance of continuing announcement of the message of Jesus in public services

Sunday by Sunday. This significance is not a matter of perpetuating a 'Christendom' in which we inappropriately seek to dominate others. It is a matter of the basic biblical truth that the worship of Yahweh is not a neutral, indifferent, private matter, but a claim that he alone is God, over against all the gods of the nations. Worship, and therefore preaching, are inescapably political acts. The attempted suppression of the voice of Christians in the former Communist countries and other places of persecution should teach us to value our opportunities and make good use of them.

The fourth and final element is the most fundamental: *the human act of communication*. Technology enables communication to happen today through many different means, and it is right that the Church should use whichever of these advance the knowledge of Christ. However, in an important respect the simple act of a person speaking to others is a form of communication that will not be superseded. This is a key difference between speech and writing, between preaching and books of theology. The person stands there as a testimony to what they are saying.[12] The words are bound up with the expression, the appearance, the whole personality. Preaching may thus be a sign and symbol of God's own means of communicating with us. His Word became flesh (John 1.14).

The other side to this, of course, is that the hearers too are called to embody the word. Those who suspect the Church of verbiage have a point if they are not able to see in the shared life of its members a living sign of the words being spoken.[13] It may be that the main effect on us of the cultural dominance of the image and the challenge to the word should not be so much the adoption of new techniques, useful as they may often be, but to focus our attention again on the importance of the life of the whole Christian community, including the preacher, in their integrity and vulnerable openness to the world as well as the word.

It is via human relationship that God and his good news are most profoundly shared, and in all the debate about contemporary forms of preaching, this truth must not be lost. Preaching is an expression of relationship. It may be formal or informal, monological or dialogical, involving images or only words. But something happens in the interaction between one human being and others with whom he or she is present which cannot be replaced by any use of technology. Here the word 'media' which has become so widespread in our language is instructive. It refers to those organs and institutions which 'mediate' information, entertainment etc. to us. These things are 'mediated' to us through them. But the opposite of 'mediated' is 'immediate'. Preaching is immediate. It is live. There is no need for 'media'. Or, putting it another way, the 'mediator' is a person. Christ is described as the 'one mediator between God and humankind' (1 Timothy 2.5) and now, in his physical absence, his disciples are sent into the world as the Father had sent him (John 20.21).

The preaching that deserves to endure is, indeed, preaching 'with humanity': a human being, *with* other humans, ready to speak words of challenge, comfort and question, yet as one of them, not set over against them. Of course, this call to 'incarnate' God applies far more widely than just to preaching: it pertains to our whole mission. We underline it here, however, to make the point that preaching, far from being the purely word-centred, cerebral act it is sometimes made out to be – in contrast, say, to 'holistic' mission embracing word, act and presence – is itself a truly 'incarnational' moment. Whether, as such, it clearly reveals God in the midst of his world will depend on whether the lives of preacher and congregation are painting the kind of picture of Christ that will be the most powerful of 'visual aids'.

Christ himself, we might say, is God 'preaching with humanity'. Through us, amazingly, he can continue to do so.

Appendix: Sermon – Luke 10.38-42

Let's face it, you and I would have been in a flap, wouldn't we? Just pottering about in the kitchen getting ready for a normal nice quiet dinner for two, a pan on the hob, your favourite cheesy dish rising nicely in the oven, and then there's a ring on the doorbell. Who is it this time? Another one of those salesmen who always seems to call just at mealtimes when he knows you'll be in? Well, it's certainly a man – you can make that out through the glass: there's his beard. But you open the door and instead it's . . . the Master. The teacher! The one you've heard so much about. The one who seems to be making waves, and calming them, wherever he goes.

But not just him. Wherever he goes, his band goes too. One, two, three – must be twelve of them – tough, hearty, hairy young men, all lining up outside the door, smiling, expectant, slightly hungry. What do you do? You can't turn the Master away. But it looks as if you don't have the Master to lunch without having his followers too. Stuttering, awkward, you beckon them in . . .

So in they come. They flop themselves down in the tiny front room. And you go into a flat spin. That cheesy dish might stretch to three, but it certainly won't stretch to fourteen. Where are the other pans? What's in the cupboard? Should you go round to the neighbour's to borrow some more dishes, to see if they've got any spare spuds? And where are we all going to sit? And what about drink? You're sure there's nothing like enough wine to go round.

In that tiny front room, so full of men, a bit sweaty from the journey, it's remarkably quiet. You suddenly stop tearing round the kitchen and cock an ear to the door. There's just one voice. The Master. He's talking. They're all listening.

But wait a moment – what about your sister, Mary? Where's she? Why's she not helping? You open the door, and there she is. In among all the men. Well, Mary . . . You gasp, not quite knowing what to say. She's listening, like them, to Jesus.

What you say then bursts out of your deepest instincts as a first-century Jewish woman. That's not a woman's place – listening to teaching! Being educated! Being with the men! A woman's place – particularly a hostess's place – is with me, in the kitchen, trying to make sure we don't mortally offend the Master and all his merry men!

'Master, don't you care that my sister has left me to serve alone?'

And you're not prepared for his response – so gentle yet so penetrating.

It seems this Jesus is not in the business of sorting out people's little family quarrels, whether it's sisters and preparing a meal or brothers and dividing an inheritance.

Instead, this Jesus wants everybody there to see the huge significance of what is taking place in that tiny house in Palestine that dusty first-century day.

'Martha, Martha, you are anxious and troubled about many things; one thing is needful. Mary has chosen the good portion, which shall not be taken away from her.'

Don't you see what Mary, your sister, has realized? By instinct – an instinct as deep as the one that led to your outburst? That really to welcome the Master goes far deeper than just laying on a meal for him and his friends, though that's important. To welcome him means to *listen to his words*.

And as you hear Jesus speaking, it dawns on you that Mary has realized something else too. That *anybody* can listen to the Master and learn from him. That it is as much a woman's place to do that as it is a man's. And then you remember hearing about some of the strange stories the Master told, with much the same message: *anybody* can do it. There was that one about a suspicious foreigner, a Samaritan, who showed he was just as capable of doing God's will and rescuing a wounded man as one of your own religious leaders – and more so. In fact, this was the kind of behaviour the Master seemed actually to draw out of people. People were talking about tax collectors giving their money away. Whatever next!

'*Anybody* can listen to me and do what I teach!'

And then it started to make sense. Your sister, squashed in among all the men. Quite naturally. A disciple along with the rest.

And you realize, as you stop there still in the doorway, transfixed by Jesus' words, just what he's saying to you. He's not saying he doesn't want your practical preparations, your diligent service, your careful cooking. He's saying he doesn't want you to be *anxious*, distracted by a multiplicity of tasks. He's saying that there is one thing, one thing above all, that will keep you on track, that will be truly *good* for you. Everything else comes from that one thing. And that one thing is *listening to him. Going on listening*, as Mary did. Going on, because there is always more to hear, more to learn, more to take in, more to obey. Out of that listening will come true service.

And you return to the kitchen, strangely quietened. Somehow that cheesy dish doesn't quite look so small any more.

Acknowledgements

Geoffrey Stevenson

'Standing on the shoulders of giants' hardly begins to express the foundation and confidence to write this book that others have given me. David Watson, David Day, Fleming Rutledge, Paul Zahl, Tony Campolo, Barbara Brown Taylor are chief among the preachers who have taken my breath away with their beautifully crafted words, even as the Holy Spirit breathed through those words. Other artists have preached the gospel to me and with me 'using words if necessary': Paul Burbridge, Director of Riding Lights Theatre Company in York knows as well as anyone the connection – and the difference – between preaching and theatre, and his friendship and wisdom have many times shaped my theatrical 'communication attempts'. I have gleefully shared several such attempts with Philip Hawthorn, actor, writer, producer and director, and now priest. Bernadette Burbridge, BBC producer and broadcaster has also encouraged and guided me both to seize unexpected opportunities and to think carefully and creatively in such moments. And how can I estimate the influence of shared dressing rooms and backstage banter with poet Stewart Henderson?

Russell-Bowman Eadie is a trainer of preachers without peer and a good friend. He Introduced me to David Schlafer, whose books I unhesitatingly recommend to those who cannot learn from him 'live'. Ron Boyd-Macmillan has been a sterling conversation partner and made invaluable comments on chapters here. Julyon Mitchell is a wise friend and constant encourager who gave me permission to work on this when the PhD he is supervising should have taken precedence! Charlie Cleverly, David Glover, Dale Hanson, Sue Hope, Phil Potter, Oliver Ross and David and Alison Wilkinson are friends who have shown me what life-long preaching ministry really looks like. Finally, I would pay tribute to my co-author, who has been a delight to write with, owing to his homiletical erudition, authorial humility, cheerful persistence, and calm efficiency. Thank you Stephen!

Stephen Wright

I am grateful to all those who, directly and indirectly, have nurtured and stimulated my preaching ministry and my reflection on the task. I recall with affection and respect the clear and compassionate preaching of the late Canon Aidan Wilson, heard weekly through much of my childhood in the parish of Morpeth, Northumberland. This strikingly illustrated the possibility of communicating the gospel mystery to all ages with simplicity but without trivialization. I am indebted to the tolerance and encouragement of congregations and colleagues in the various parishes where I have served as a priest in some capacity or other: in Cumbria, St Paul, Barrow-in-Furness, and Holme and Burton; in County Durham, Esh and Hamsteels, and Consett; and now in South London, St John the Divine, Selsdon. Since 1998 I have greatly appreciated the rich ecumenical fellowship of the College of Preachers and the insights and support received within it – from many, whom it would be invidious to start to name. I was grateful to its Executive Committee for the sabbatical from my post as Director of the college in 2005 when some of the initial work for this book was done. Over these recent years I have been based at Spurgeon's College, London, a generous and hospitable environment for developing the study and practice of preaching, where I have learned and received much from a diverse range of colleagues and students – again, too many to name here. The experience has underlined my conviction that no single tradition within the Christian family has all the wisdom on preaching (or indeed on anything else), and that preaching itself can be the focus for the sharing of such wisdom across the traditions. It has been a privilege to work with Geoffrey on this project. I have learned much from his unique talents and experience and the way that he uses them in the service of proclaiming God's kingdom.

We both want especially to thank Kathryn Pritchard of Church House Publishing for her enthusiasm, commitment and clear-eyed guidance in this venture. We remain, of course, solely responsible for the views expressed.

Resources

This is far from being an exhaustive list of the many useful books and other resources which are available to support the ministry of preaching. We have tried to offer a representative selection, arranged by themes roughly corresponding to the chapters in this book, though inevitably many items might be placed in more than one category.

Preaching – general

Roger Bowen, *A Guide to Preaching*, SPCK, 2005

Ronald Boyd-MacMillan, *Explosive Preaching: Letters on detonating the gospel in the 21st century*, Paternoster Press, 2005

R. E. C. Browne, *The Ministry of the Word*, SCM Press, 1976

F. D. Coggan, *A New Day for Preaching: The sacrament of the word*, SPCK, 1996

Fred B. Craddock, *Preaching*, Abingdon Press, 1985

David Day, *Embodying the Word: A preacher's guide*, SPCK, 2005

David Day, *A Preaching Workbook*, new edn, SPCK, 2004

David Day, Jeff Astley and Leslie J. Francis (eds), *A Reader on Preaching: Making connections*, Ashgate, 2005

Thomas G. Long, *The Witness of Preaching*, 2nd ed., Westminster John Knox Press, 2005

Michael J. Quicke, *360-Degree Preaching: Hearing, speaking, and living the word*, Baker Academic / Paternoster Press, 2003

John R.W. Stott, *I Believe in Preaching*, Hodder and Stoughton, 1982

Paul Scott Wilson, *The Practice of Preaching*, 2nd edn, Abingdon Press, 2007

See also the College of Preachers: www.collegeofpreachers.org.uk

(The College of Preachers arranges a variety of training events, publishes a quarterly journal and offers online resources and DVD material for the development of preachers and preaching.)

Preaching in mission to contemporary culture (chapters 1 and 10)

Walter Brueggemann, *Texts under Negotiation: The Bible and postmodern imagination*, Fortress Press, 1993

Shane Hipps, *The Hidden Power of Electronic Culture: How media shapes faith, the gospel and church*, Zondervan, 2005

Graham Johnston, *Preaching to a Postmodern World*, IVP, 2001

David J. Lose, *Confessing Jesus Christ: Preaching in a postmodern world*, William B. Eerdmans, 2003

Jolyon P. Mitchell, *Visually Speaking: Radio and the renaissance of preaching*, T&T Clark, 1999

Stuart Murray, 'Interactive Preaching', in *Evangel*,17:2 (Summer 1999), pp. 53–7

Doug Pagitt, *Preaching Re-imagined: The role of the sermon in communities of faith*, Zondervan, 2005

The liturgical context of preaching (chapters 1 and 2)

Anne Barton, *All-Age Worship*, Grove Books, 1993

Richard St L. Broadberry, 'Preaching to Children within the Context of All-Age Worship', *College of Preachers Journal*, No.119 (July 2005), pp. 7–13, with responses by Judy Jarvis (pp. 14–16) and Peter Privett (pp. 17–20)

John E. Colwell, *The Rhythm of Doctrine: A liturgical sketch of Christian faith and faithfulness*, Paternoster Press, 2007

Marva J. Dawn, *Reaching out without Dumbing Down: A theology of worship for the turn-of-the-century culture*, William B. Eerdmans, 1995

Reginald H. Fuller, *What is Liturgical Preaching?*, SCM Press, 1957

Tim Stratford, *Interactive Preaching: Opening the word then listening*, Grove Books, 1998

Phillip Tovey, *Preaching a Sermon Series with Common Worship*, Grove Books, 2004

The educational context of preaching (chapters 1 and 10)

D. S. Cunningham, *To Teach, to Delight, and to Move: Theological education in a post-Christian world*, Cascade Books, 2004

D. C. Norrington, *To Preach or Not to Preach?*, Paternoster Press, 1996

Jeremy Thomson, *Preaching as Dialogue: Is the sermon a sacred cow?*, Grove Books, 1996

The pastoral context of preaching (chapters 1 and 2)

Paul Ballard, and John Pritchard, *Practical Theology in Action*, 2nd edn, SPCK, 2006

John Pritchard, *The Life and Work of a Priest*, SPCK, 2007

Michael J. Quicke, *360-degree Leadership: Preaching to transform congregations*, Baker Book House, 2006

'Black' preaching (chapter 2)

Joe Aldred, *Preaching with Power: Sermons by black preachers*, Cassell, 1998

Joe Aldred, *Sisters with Power*, Continuum, 2000

Henry H. Mitchell, *Black Preaching: The recovery of a powerful art*, Abingdon Press, 1991

The theology of preaching (chapter 3)

Karl Barth, *Homiletics*, trans. G. W. Bromiley and D. E. Daniels, Westminster John Knox Press, 1991

Jana Childers (ed.), *Purposes of Preaching*, Chalice Press, 2004

Mary Katherine Hilkert, *Naming Grace: Preaching and the sacramental imagination*, Continuum, 1997

Michael Pasquarello III, *Christian Preaching: A trinitarian theology of proclamation*, Baker Academic, 2006

Lucy Atkinson Rose, *Sharing the Word: Preaching in the roundtable church*, Westminster John Knox Press, 1997

The person of the preacher (chapters 4 and 8)

Susan Durber, *Preaching Like a Woman*, SPCK, 2007

Mike Graves, *The Fully Alive Preacher: Recovering from homiletical burnout*, Westminster John Knox Press, 2006

Richard Lischer, *Open Secrets: A memoir of faith and discovery*, Doubleday, 2001

A. Mehrabian, *Silent Messages: Implicit communication of emotions and attitudes*, Wadsworth Publishing, 1971

Geoffrey Stevenson, *Pulpit Journeys*, Darton, Longman & Todd, 2006

Barbara Brown Taylor, *Leaving Church: A memoir of faith*, Harper Collins, 2007

Barbara Brown Taylor, *When God Is Silent*, Cowley Publications,1998

The Bible and interpretation in preaching (chapter 5)

David G. Buttrick, 'The Use of the Bible in Preaching', in Leander E. Keck (ed.), *The New Interpreter's Bible*, vol.1, Abingdon Press, 1994, pp. 188–99

Ellen F. Davis, *Wondrous Depth: Preaching the Old Testament*, Westminster John Knox Press, 2005

Stephen Farris, *Preaching that Matters: The Bible and our lives*, Westminster John Knox Press, 1998

John Goldingay, *Models for Interpretation of Scripture*, William B. Eerdmans/ Paternoster Press, 1995

Sidney P. Greidanus, *The Modern Preacher and the Ancient Text*, William B. Eerdmans, 1988

Paul Scott Wilson, *God Sense: Reading the Bible for preaching*, Abingdon Press, 2001

Stephen I. Wright, *Preaching with the Grain of Scripture*, Grove Books, 2001

Sermon structures (chapter 6)

Richard L. Eslinger, *The Web of Preaching*, Abingdon Press, 2002

Mike Graves, *The Sermon as Symphony: Preaching the literary forms of the New Testament*, Judson Press, 1997

Thomas G. Long, *Preaching and the Literary Forms of the Bible*, Augsburg Fortress, 1988

Eugene L. Lowry, *The Sermon: Dancing the edge of mystery*, Abingdon Press, 1997

Thomas H. Troeger, *Imagining a Sermon*, Abingdon Press, 1993

Storytelling and narrative preaching (chapters 6 and 7)

W. J. Bausch, *Storytelling: Imagination and faith*, Twenty-Third Publications, 1984

Thomas E. Boomershine, *Story Journey: An invitation to the gospel as storytelling*, Abingdon Press, 1988

Peter Brooks, *Communicating Conviction*, Epworth Press, 1983

Richard L. Eslinger, *Narrative Imagination: Preaching the worlds that shape us*, Fortress Press, 1995

G. Robert Jacks, *Just Say the Word: Writing for the ear*, William B. Eerdmans, 1996

Richard Littledale, *Stale Bread? Refreshing the preaching ministry*, St Andrew Press, 2007

Eugene L. Lowry, *How to Preach a Parable: Designs for narrative sermons*, Abingdon Press, 1990

Calvin Miller, *Preaching: The art of narrative exposition*, Baker Books, 2006

Nina Rosenstand, *The Moral of the Story*, 4th edn, McGraw Hill, 2003

Roger Standing, *Finding the Plot: Preaching in a narrative style*, Paternoster Press, 2004

William R. White, *Speaking in Stories*, Augsburg Press, 1982

See also

The Network of Biblical Storytellers: email: nobsint@nobs.org; web site: www.nobs.org

Dennis Dewey, Biblical storyteller: www.dennisdewey.org

Storytelling booklist: http://www.timsheppard.co.uk/story

Voice care and speech (chapter 7)

Cicely Berry, *Voice and the Actor*, John Wiley & Sons, 1991

Cicely Berry, *Your Voice and How to Use It*, Virgin, 2000

Greta Colson, *Voice Production and Speech*, Longman, 1998

B. Houseman, *Finding Your Voice: A complete voice training manual for actors*, Nick Hern Books, 2002

Evangeline Machlin, *Speech for the Stage*, Routledge, 1993

Ken Parkin, *An Anthology of British Tongue Twisters*, Samuel French Ltd, 1969

Patsy Rodenburg, *The Right to Speak: Working with the voice*, Methuen Drama, 1992

Patsy Rodenburg, video: *A Voice of Your Own*, Vanguard Productions, PO Box 70, Norwich NR1 2ED.

Peter Westland, *Public Speaking (Teach Yourself)*, Hodder & Stoughton, 1976

Reading and presentation (chapters 7 and 8)

Jana Childers, *Performing the Word: Preaching as theatre*, Abingdon Press, 1998

G. Robert Jacks, *Getting the Word Across: Speech communication for pastors and lay leaders*, William B. Eerdmans, 1995

T. R. B. Hodgson, *Saying the Services*, Churchman Publishing,1989

Anna de Lange and Liz Simpson, *How to . . . Read the Bible in Church*, Grove Books, 2003

Methodist Church, *The Worship Leader's Training Pack*, Methodist Publishing House

Wendy Palmer, *Reading from the Front* and *Speaking from the Front*, audio cassette and booklet from: Wendy Palmer, 22 Duffield Court, Chapel St, Duffield, Derbyshire DE56

Joseph John Parker, *Guidance for Readers: A handbook for those who read at Mass*, NDLC, The Liturgy of the Word Dept, St John Bosco Presbytery, 88 Paisley Road, Leicester LE2 9BU, 1999

Clayton J. Schmit, *Public Reading of Scripture*, Abingdon Press, 2002

Working with the congregation (chapter 9)

Mark Greene, *The Three-Eared Preacher*, London Bible College, 1998

John S. McClure, *The Roundtable Pulpit*, Abingdon Press, 1995

David J. Schlafer, *Playing with Fire: Preaching work as kindling art*, Cowley Publications, 2004

Leonora Tubbs Tisdale, *Preaching as Local Theology and Folk Art*, Fortress Press, 1997

Roger Van Harn, *Preacher, Can You Hear Us Listening?*, William B. Eerdmans, 1992

Notes

Prelude

1   The Second Helvetic Confession was written by Heinrich Bullinger in 1561.

Chapter 1 The problems with 'preaching'

1   See, for instance, the Lambeth Conference 1988 Resolution 44, calling for 'a shift to a dynamic missionary emphasis, going beyond care and nurture to proclamation and service': cited in *Mission-shaped Church: Church planting and fresh expressions of church in a changing context*, Church House Publishing, 2004.

2   *Mission-shaped Church*.

3   *Mission-shaped Church*, p. 101.

4   Pete Ward, 'The role of preaching at a time of fast cultural change', interview with Stuart Blythe, *The Preacher: The College of Preachers' Journal*, No. 121, April 2006, pp. 9, 10.

5   See, for instance, Jolyon P. Mitchell, *Visually Speaking: Radio and the renaissance of preaching*, T&T Clark, 1999.

6   For a very helpful overview of how the shift to electronic culture relates to developments in Christian worship, see Shane Hipps, *The Hidden Power of Electronic Culture: How media shapes faith, the gospel and church*, Zondervan, 2005.

7   This was by no means a new perception of preaching in the history of the Church; but it was given careful expression at this time by R. H. Fuller in his book *What is Liturgical Preaching?*, SCM Press, 1957.

8   These two paragraphs are taken from an article by the author (Stephen Wright), 'Giving Voice to the Word: Reflections on the College of Preachers 1960–2005', *Epworth Review*, vol. 32 no. 3, July 2005, pp. 39–46.

9   Leslie Griffiths, 'Preaching: a dying art?', *The Reader*, Spring 2006, pp. 2, 3.

10 Joanna Cox, 'Readers – learning to help others to learn', *The Reader*, Spring 2006, pp. 17, 18, 29. 'Readers' are lay ministers in the Church of England, authorized to preach, teach and undertake pastoral duties but not to preside at the Holy Communion.

11 Fred B. Craddock, *Preaching*, Abingdon Press, 1985, p. 167.

12 Thomas G. Long, *The Witness of Preaching*, 2nd edn, Westminster John Knox Press, 2005, pp. 3–8.

13 Leonora Tubbs Tisdale, *Preaching as Local Theology and Folk Art*, Fortress Press, 1997.

14 John S. McClure, *The Roundtable Pulpit*, Abingdon Press, 1995.

15 David J. Schlafer, *Playing with Fire: Preaching work as kindling art*, Cowley Publications, 2004, pp. 133–48.

16 Griffiths, 'Preaching: a dying art?', p. 3.

17 For a helpful statement of this see Paul Ballard and John Pritchard, *Practical Theology in Action*, 2nd edn, SPCK, 2006, pp. 51–2.

18 The relationship between preaching and leadership is hotly debated in some quarters, especially in North America. See Michael J. Quicke, *360-Degree Leadership: Preaching to transform congregations*, Baker Book House, 2006.

Chapter 2 Preaching in worship today

1 See the classic, though now dated, study of R. H. Fuller, *What is Liturgical Preaching?*, SCM Press, 1957.

2 See C. H. Dodd, *The Apostolic Preaching and its Developments*, Hodder & Stoughton, 1936, p. 7. The sharpness of Dodd's distinction between various types of 'preaching' in the New Testament, including 'teaching', is however open to question.

3 John Stott, *I Believe in Preaching*, Hodder & Stoughton, 1982, p. 126.

4 This style of preaching was known as *homilia*, from the Greek for 'conversation'. This does not necessarily imply a lack of preparation by the preacher – but it does suggest that the sermon is simply a 'conversation' about the text, which in principle could happen in a very informal way. Confusingly, the word 'homily' nowadays tends to suggest brevity and is associated with the 'liturgical preaching' tradition, rather than with this idea of a leisurely conversation over a text; but this fact does underline the importance of Scripture for liturgical preaching too, and that tradition's link with the Early Church.

5 See the fascinating exploration of Christian doctrine through the lens of the Christian year (interestingly, from the pen of a Baptist) by John Colwell, *The Rhythm of Doctrine: A liturgical sketch of Christian faith and faithfulness*, Paternoster, 2007.

6 I have learned much from my colleagues Tim Grass and Chris Voke about this tradition.

7 See Henry H. Mitchell, *Black Preaching: The recovery of a powerful art*, Abingdon Press, 1991; Joe Aldred, *Preaching with Power: Sermons by black preachers*, Cassell, 1998; *Sisters with Power*, Continuum, 2000.

8 See Marva J. Dawn, *Reaching out without Dumbing Down: A theology of worship for the turn-of-the-century culture*, Eerdmans, 1995; Richard St L. Broadberry, 'Preaching to Children within the Context of All-Age Worship', *College of Preachers Journal*, No. 119, July 2005, pp. 7–13, with responses by Judy Jarvis (pp. 14–16) and Peter Privett (pp. 17–20).

9 See the useful treatment by Anne Barton, *All-Age Worship*, Grove, 1993.

10 I am grateful to Ron Boyd-Macmillan for drawing my attention to the link between Tillotson and Williams. Cf. Rowan Williams' collection of sermons, *Open to Judgement*, Darton, Longman & Todd, 1994.

11 Such an approach was eloquently advocated by the late Bishop Lesslie Newbigin.

Chapter 3 The players in preaching

1 See Karl Barth, *Church Dogmatics, 1.1: The Doctrine of the Word of God*, trans. G. W. Bromiley, T&T Clark International, 2004. [reprint of 2nd edn 1975]

2 Janet Proctor, MTh Dissertation, Spurgeon's College and the College of Preachers, 2006.

3 Roger Van Harn, *Pew Rights: For people who listen to sermons*, Eerdmans, 1992, pp. 155–9.

4 See Thomas G. Long, *The Witness of Preaching*, 2nd edn, Westminster John Knox Press, 2005, pp. 3–8.

5 See Ernesto Cardenal, *The Gospel in Solentiname*, Orbis Books, 1982.

6 See especially Long, *The Witness of Preaching*, pp. 45–51. David J. Lose mounts a similar argument for the word 'confession' as a helpful summary of the preacher's role today: *Confessing Jesus Christ: Preaching in a postmodern world*, Eerdmans, 2003.

7 Phillips Brooks, *Lectures on Preaching*, Macmillan, 1903, p. 5.

Chapter 4 The human preacher

1 Phillips Brooks, *The Joy of Preaching (1877): Foreword and biographical information by Warren Wiersbe*, Kregel Publications, 1989, p. 27.

2 Brooks, *The Joy of Preaching*, pp. 47–60.

3 Fred B. Craddock, *Preaching*, Abingdon Press, 1985, p. 24.

4 Michael J. Quicke, *360-Degree Preaching: Hearing, speaking, and living the word*, Baker Academic/Paternoster, p. 94.

5 Ronald Boyd-Macmillan, *Explosive Preaching: Letters on detonating the gospel in the 21st century*, Paternoster, 2005, p. 59.

6 There is more on self-disclosure in the pulpit later in this chapter.

7 I owe this insight to Professor Oliver O'Donovan and his homiletics lectures in 2007 to students at New College, Edinburgh.

8 I owe these first three headings (and much else) to my friend and colleague David Day, who develops them profoundly and insightfully in his excellent *Embodying the Word*, SPCK, 2005.

9 Day, *Embodying the Word*, p. 14.

10 Barbara Brown Taylor, *When God Is Silent*, Cowley Publications, 1998, p. 80.

11 Craddock, *Preaching*, p. 55.

12 Calvin Miller, *Preaching: The art of narrative exposition*, Baker, 2006, p. 38.

13 Richard Lischer, *Open Secrets: A memoir of faith and discovery*, Doubleday, 2001.

14 John Pritchard, *The Life and Work of a Priest*, SPCK, 2007.

15 They are particularly important to help with the issue of work–life balance that troubles ministers as much as anyone else. Indeed, because they believe themselves called to be servants, they can find it impossible to say no to the pressing, heart-breaking needs that are always just outside their front door.

16 Eugene L. Lowry, *The Sermon: Dancing the edge of mystery*, Abingdon Press, 1997.

17 Richard L. Eslinger, *The Web of Preaching*, Abingdon Press, 2002.

18 See Walter Brueggemann, *Texts under Negotiation: The Bible and postmodern imagination*, Fortress Press, 1993.

19 In fact the exact source for this quote has not been found, as far as Princeton Seminary's Center for Barth Studies is concerned. On their web site they note, 'Perhaps the most clear statement on the record from Barth concerning these matters comes from a Time Magazine piece on Barth published on Friday, May 31, 1963. "[Barth] recalls that 40 years ago he advised young theologians 'to take your Bible and take your newspaper, and read both. But interpret newspapers from your Bible.' " '

20 John Claypool, 'Life is a Gift', in Thomas G. Long and Cornelius Plantinga, Jr (eds), *A Chorus of Witnesses: Model sermons for today's preacher*, Eerdmans, 1994, pp. 120–30.

21 Claypool, 'Life is a Gift', p. 123.

22 Claypool, 'Life is a Gift', p. 130.

Chapter 5 The go-between preacher

1 See William J. Abraham, *Canon and Criterion in Christian Theology: From the fathers to feminism*, Oxford University Press, 2002.

2 Augustine of Hippo set a great example here. See C. Clifton Black, 'Augustinian Preaching and the Nurture of Christians', in Roger E. Van Harn (ed.), *The Lectionary Commentary: Theological exegesis for Sunday's texts*, Eerdmans, 2001, vol. 3 (The Gospels), pp. 603–14.

3 Cited in David G. Buttrick, 'The Use of the Bible in Preaching', in Leander E. Keck (ed.), *The New Interpreter's Bible*, vol. 1, Abingdon Press, 1994, pp. 188–99 (p. 190).

4 For a classic account of this process see Hans Frei, *The Eclipse of Biblical Narrative*, Yale University Press, 1974.

5 I owe this usage to Professor Michael Quicke.

6 See the helpful ideas for devising sermon series based on the *Common Worship* Lectionary in Phillip Tovey, *Preaching a Sermon Series with Common Worship*, Grove Books, 2004.

7 Joel B. Green, *The Gospel of Luke*, The New International Commentary on the New Testament, Eerdmans, 1997.

8 See, for example, the work of Old Testament scholar and preacher Walter Brueggemann, in both his theological writings and his published sermons.

9 Here, of course, I was reading between the lines: this is inevitable in interpreting Scripture, and I believe that one of the advantages of a more oblique, narrative format for a sermon is that it allows one to do so without claiming that this is the only way to read the biblical story.

10 Fred B. Craddock, *Preaching*, Abingdon Press, 1985, p. 120.

11 This seems a good place to acknowledge that as authors we are aware of the inevitable one-sidedness of this book itself, written as it is from a male perspective, and to express great regret that our co-author Alison Wilkinson had to withdraw from the project due to ill-health. We cannot begin to deal here with the vital questions raised by a consideration of preaching in the light of gender. For one of the most up-to-date treatments of preaching from a female perspective see Susan Durber, *Preaching Like a Woman*, SPCK, 2007.

12 Again here I must acknowledge the seminal influence of Craddock's *Preaching* on my thinking, especially in the language of 'negotiating the distance' between the text and the listeners (pp. 125–50).

Chapter 6 Preparing to preach

1 This is a central feature of what has been dubbed 'the New Homiletic' in North America. In the UK there have been welcome signs of a fresh interest and burst of creativity in thinking about sermon forms and shapes, much of which has been influenced by American writers such as Fred Craddock and Eugene Lowry. See particularly Jolyon P. Mitchell, *Visually Speaking: Radio and the renaissance of preaching*, T&T Clark, 1999; Roger Standing, *Finding the Plot: Preaching in a narrative style*, Paternoster Press, 2004; David Day, *Embodying the Word: A preacher's guide*, SPCK, 2005; Ronald Boyd-Macmillan, *Explosive Preaching: Letters on detonating the gospel in the 21st century*, Paternoster Press, 2005; Richard Littledale, *Stale Bread? Refreshing the preaching ministry*, St Andrew Press, 2007. It is interesting that these writers cross something of the denominational spectrum. Those who wish to explore different sermon structures in more detail will find plenty of inspiration and ideas here, as I have done myself.

2 In my booklet *Preaching with the Grain of Scripture*, Grove Books, 2001, I tried to open up the subject of sermon structures which stay close to the thrust of the text; there was not space to explore the equally important dimensions of structures which 'fit' the occasion and the hearers.

3 There are all sorts of ways to go about this, which we haven't space to explore here. See especially Eugene L. Lowry, *How to Preach a Parable*, Abingdon Press,

1989, Standing, *Finding the Plot*; Littledale, *Stale Bread*. It is especially interesting to weigh up the pros and cons of the use of the different pronouns in a narrative approach. In my sermon I adopted the rather unusual tactic (for me at least) of using 'you'.

4   See Thomas G. Long, *Preaching and the Literary Forms of the Bible*, Augsburg Fortress, 1988; Mike Graves, *The Sermon as Symphony: Preaching the literary forms of the New Testament*, Judson Press, 1997.

5   See also Ron Boyd-Macmillan's very helpful book, *Explosive Preaching*.

6   Preachers who are blind or partially sighted are a special and important exception here.

7   This view is central to the approach of Fred Craddock in *Preaching*, Abingdon Press, 1985.

Chapter 7 The act of delivery

1   K. S. Stanislavski, *An Actor Prepares*, trans. E. R. Hapgood, Geoffrey Bles, 1937.

2   Especially recommended is W. J. Bausch, *Storytelling: Imagination and faith*, Twenty-Third Publications, 1984.

3   Jana Childers, *Performing the Word: Preaching as theatre*, Abingdon Press, 1998, p. 60.

4   Childers, *Performing the Word*, p. 60.

5   This line contains the range of vowel sounds sometimes referred to as the Resonator Scale.

6   I am grateful to Speech and Language Therapist Jayne Comins for teaching me several of these exercises and voice care techniques.

7   See the Resources section, pp. 129–34.

Chapter 8 Communication and communion

1   D. Day, *Embodying the Word: A preacher's guide*, SPCK, 2004.

2   The most common exception to this is what used to be known in some circles as 'tape ministry' but which now can spread the preacher's words by CD, DVD, podcasts and YouTube™.

3   A. Mehrabian, *Silent Messages: Implicit communication of emotions and attitudes*, Wadsworth Publishing, 1971, pp. 43–4.

4   Bert Decker, *The Art of Communicating*, Thomas Crisp Learning, 1996, p. 35.

5   Thomas Hardy, 'In Church', from *Satires of Circumstance in Fifteen Glimpses* (1914).

6   See his excellent book on rhetoric: D. S. Cunningham, *To Teach, to Delight, and to Move: Theological education in a post-Christian world*, Cascade Books, 2004.

7   Preaching in that situation has its drawbacks, since there is no one direction in

which to face, and you can end up wheeling around in circles trying to make eye contact with everybody.

8   Current UK products dedicated to worship include Visual Liturgy Live, Presentation Manager 6, Songbase and SongPro v. 4. OpenSong (www.opensong.org) is a free, open source application, and by no means the only free one at the time of writing. The 'open source' alternative to PowerPoint™ is called Impress.

9   Iconoclasm and the stormy and contradictory relationship the Church has had with images historically have been connected by historical theologians with the deep desire of the laity to have some pictures to be going on with even though they are not needed by educated, cerebral clergy. Protestants still privilege the word and may even today carry with them something of the zeal of the Reformers to repudiate Catholicism by destroying image-based practices of worship. This reminds me of the Israelites whom Moses caught *in flagrante delicto* with some calf-shaped gold. But I would maintain that images are not in themselves intrinsically idolatrous.

Chapter 9 Preaching in community – the sermon as expression of the congregation

1   This is not to rule out sermon forms that employ conversation or dialogue or structured or unstructured exchanges between different voices.

2   Thomas G. Long, *The Witness of Preaching*, 2nd edn, Westminster John Knox Press, 2005, p. 11.

3   But we will not pause here to consider the full extent of the implication arising from this understanding of the sermon for a preacher's calling and ordination.

4   Mark Greene in *The Three Eared Preacher*, London Bible College, 1998, explores this concept in depth and the book contains sample surveys to be used. For congregations that may be resistant to questionnaires, Leonora Tubbs Tisdale develops alternative ways of 'exegeting the congregation' in her *Preaching as Local Theology and Folk Art*, Augsburg Press, 1997. These are part of a growing literature on congregational studies that preachers should make part of their own study.

5   J. S. McClure, *The Roundtable Pulpit: Where leadership and preaching meet*, Abingdon Press, 1995, esp. pp. 59–72. The idea is also developed by David Schlafer with his Preaching Discernment Groups, see David J. Schlafer, *Playing with Fire: Preaching work as kindling art*, Cowley Publications, 2004, pp. 140ff.

6   Ronald Boyd-Macmillan, *Explosive Preaching: Letters on detonating the gospel in the 21st century*, Paternoster, 2006, pp. 182–3.

7   Every student of preaching should acknowledge the force of the criticisms of preaching as a mode of teaching, forcefully expressed in D. C. Norrington, *To Preach or Not to Preach?*, Paternoster Press, 1996.

8   David J. Schlafer, *Surviving the Sermon: A guide to preaching for those who have to listen*, Cowley Publications, 1992, p. 63.

9 Schlafer, *Surviving the Sermon*, p. 64.

10 David J. Schlafer, *Your Way with God's Word*, Cowley Publications, 1995, p. 57.

11 For more on congregational feedback, see Paul Ballard and John Pritchard, *Practical Theology in Action*, 2nd edn, SPCK, 2006, and note for instance the sermon evaluation form given on pp. 201–2.

12 Geoffrey Stevenson, *Pulpit Journeys*, Darton, Longman & Todd, 2006, p. 52.

13 http://whengodsvoiceisheard.blogspot.com/

Chapter 10 Preaching in a mission-conscious Church

1 It is interesting that the 'Notes' to the Church of England's Holy Communion service in *Common Worship* include the following rubric: 'The sermon may on occasion include less formal exposition of Scripture, the use of drama, interviews, discussion and audio-visual aids': *Common Worship: Services and prayers for the Church of England*, Church House Publishing, 2000, p. 332.

2 See D. C. Norrington, *To Preach or Not to Preach?*, Paternoster Press, 1996; Stuart Murray, 'Interactive Preaching', in *Evangel* 17.2 (Summer 1999), pp. 53–7; Jeremy Thomson, *Preaching as Dialogue: Is the sermon a sacred cow?*, Grove Books, 1996; Tim Stratford, *Interactive Preaching: Opening the word then listening*, Grove Books, 1998.

3 Such meetings are described, for instance, in the report *Mission-shaped Church: Church planting and fresh expressions of church in a changing context*, Church House Publishing, 2004.

4 Stratford, *Interactive Preaching*.

5 Norrington, *To Preach*; Murray, 'Interactive Preaching'.

6 Thomson, *Preaching as Dialogue*.

7 Michael J. Quicke, *360-Degree Leadership: Preaching to transform congregations*, Baker Book House, 2006.

8 Cited in William J. Abraham, *Canon and Criterion in Christian Theology*, Oxford University Press, 1998, p. 52.

9 I first heard this point made by Ian Paton, Vicar of Old St Paul's, Edinburgh.

10 Apart from works cited earlier in the book, see R. E. C. Browne, *The Ministry of the Word*, SCM Press, 1976; Thomas H. Troeger, *Imagining a Sermon*, Abingdon Press, 1993.

11 This is a point on which Lesslie Newbigin's appeal to the Churches to adopt a 'missionary' stance to our Western culture was particularly based.

12 I am grateful to Bishop James Jones for making this point with particular force.

13 Cf. Lesslie Newbigin's now justly famous comment: 'the only effective hermeneutic [i.e. interpretation] of the gospel is the life of the congregation which believes it' (*The Gospel in a Pluralist Society*, SPCK, 1989, p. 234).

General index

Note: Where endnotes for more than chapter appear on one page, the sequences
are distinguished by the addition of a, b or c to the note number.

Index of biblical references